To Hans,
Do share
stories!

My
MUSIC MAN

Dede Montgomery

My MUSIC MAN

Dede Montgomery

BInk *Bink Books*
Bedazzled Ink Publishing Company • Fairfield, California

paperback 978-1-945805-41-7

Cover Design
by

DESIGNS

Bink Books
a division of
Bedazzled Ink Publishing, LLC
Fairfield, California
http://www.bedazzledink.com

For Dad. I love you as big as the whole sky.

Acknowledgements

I wish to thank many people for their help in creating this book.

Claudia, Casey, and the team at Bedazzled Ink Books for taking a chance in me and with my book. Erin Axelrod as my developmental editor, and for her skill and patience as she helped teach me to become a better writer. Patty Montgomery for spending hundreds of hours putting together the volumes and volumes of photos and stories about Dad's family. My brothers, Patrick, Andrew, Michael, and Rick, for leaving me with so many "brother stories," and especially Patrick for sharing his earliest river memories. Erin, Emily, and my nieces for allowing me to share some stories of their childhood. Willamette University Research Library, Oregon Historical Society, Oregon History Museum, and the Museum of the Oregon Territory for preserving and advocating public access to history. My dear friends and family who kindly read my manuscript and offered insights and tips, including Jeanne Finley, Karen Bonoff, Karen Lennon, Kermit McCarthy, Maura Doherty, Katie and Louis Barker, Elizabeth Rocchia, Ann Clark, and Gordon Gregory. And finally, I thank Russell for beautifying my family tree and putting up with late nights, early mornings, and repetitive blasting of the Irish Tenors.

Table of Contents

Family Tree   9
Chapter 1: Lover of Rivers   13
Chapter 2: Snow and Ice   20
Chapter 3: Baseball   27
Chapter 4: Summer   35
Chapter 5: Heartstrings   42
Chapter 6: The Falls   55
Chapter 7: Dangerous Living   68
Chapter 8: Our Town   75
Chapter 9: Monkey Wrenching   83
Chapter 10: Boats, Carp and Steamers   89
Chapter 11: Pirates   103
Chapter 12: Girl in a Boys' World   117
Chapter 13: Champoeg   126
Chapter 14: Floods, Earthquakes, and Volcanoes   131
Chapter 15: Chemeketa   137
Chapter 16: Books   145
Chapter 17: Interrupted   153
Chapter 18: My Titan   161
Chapter 19: Watching the River Run   174
Afterward: The Writing of this Book   179
Sources   183

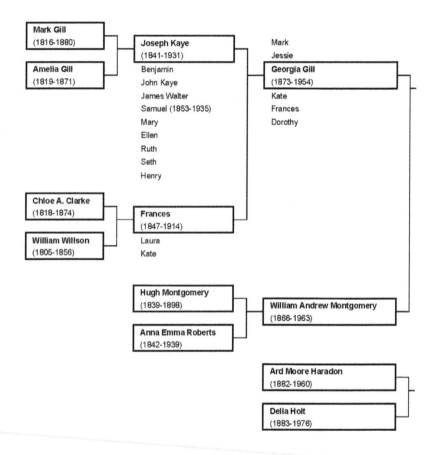

Mark Gill
(1816-1880)

Amelia Gill
(1819-1871)

Joseph Kaye
(1841-1931)
Benjamin
John Kaye
James Walter
Samuel (1853-1935)
Mary
Ellen
Ruth
Seth
Henry

Mark
Jessie
Georgia Gill
(1873-1954)
Kate
Frances
Dorothy

Chloe A. Clarke
(1818-1874)

William Willson
(1805-1856)

Frances
(1847-1914)
Laura
Kate

Hugh Montgomery
(1839-1898)

Anna Emma Roberts
(1842-1939)

William Andrew Montgomery
(1866-1963)

Ard Moore Haradon
(1882-1960)

Delia Holt
(1883-1976)

Family Tree

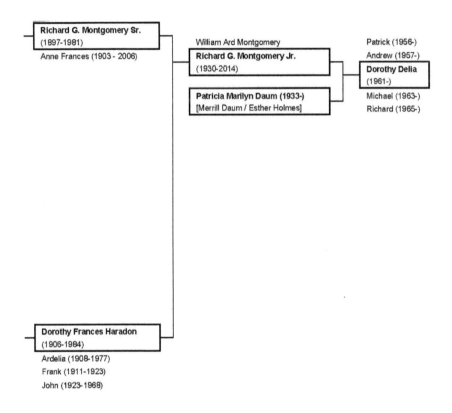

Richard G. Montgomery Sr.
(1897-1981)
Anne Frances (1903 - 2006)

William Ard Montgomery
Richard G. Montgomery Jr.
(1930-2014)

Patricia Marilyn Daum (1933-)
[Merrill Daum / Esther Holmes]

Patrick (1956-)
Andrew (1957-)
Dorothy Delia
(1961-)
Michael (1963-)
Richard (1965-)

Dorothy Frances Haradon
(1906-1984)
Ardelia (1908-1977)
Frank (1911-1923)
John (1923-1968)

CHAPTER 1
A LOVER OF RIVERS

IT WAS BECAUSE of the tanneries that we didn't build my childhood house on Oregon's Tualatin River. The real deal breaker, said our dad to Uncle Bill. In truth, the decision to put money down to build on the banks of our valley's neighboring Willamette River may have been more about the memories imprinted in Dad's brain from his childhood. To build the only house he ever lived in that was built from scratch and moved into new.

Oh my. The Willamette. What is it to be of the Willamette River? Its banks create smells for each season. As the days grow shorter and fall's dense chill sets in, smoke from fireplaces and field burning mingle with rotting leaves. Pumpkins ripen on the vine, their stems curling toward the earth. We kids quickly claim which giant squash will be our selection, to be honed by knife as our Halloween masterpiece. We savor the last of our stunted daylight hours.

Dede, Dickie and Mike, 1968

When I was six, my neighbor, Frank, born over half a century before me just at the turn of the century, pulled out a shovel to help me dig new russet potatoes, brown and knobby, from his garden. Mostly bald-headed, Frank Lockyear wore an old Boy Scout jamboree T-shirt, I guess reflective of decades of working with scouts. Frank was a nurseryman who believed the world needed more trees, and in his lifetime, organized the planting of millions of trees in the Pacific Northwest and dozens of countries around the world. Frank's name is left behind in a memorial grove of trees that he planted in 1934 near Oregon's Clackamas River. He has one of those smiles that turned his whole face into layers of crinkles. My own dad—a handsome, strong guy who looked a bit like those good-looking magazine models if you ignored the profile of his nose that he had broken a couple of times— liked cutting down trees, bucking up logs, and mowing grass. But Frank toiled in his vegetable garden, inspired to show me his rows of late season carrots. His garden was even bigger than our mom's. Hers with rows of fat green peas earlier in the summer but now missing asparagus to cut back because my older brother, Andy, overzealously weeded them out.

But Frank's garden was huge! He patiently showed me all that was still popping out of our rich valley earth, even as the days shortened. Rows of carrots and mounds of squash plants overtaken by their rough, now yellowed, withering leaves. He didn't like me to call him Mr. Lockyear, so he was just Frank. We wrapped the just-out-of-the-earth potatoes in foil, burying them deep into the ashes of the bonfire simmering in his several-acred front yard. While we awaited our snack on this Willamette Valley fall day, he let me dash between his garden rows—many of them now turned under and renewed with compost. I showed him how little I was by climbing into the cardboard box, lying in wait of filling from the remainder of his garden's offerings. He took a picture, me with legs hanging over the box edge, and told me he'd send it to my mom so she would know where I had been.

And then, our potatoes were cooked. Frank used a long metal rake to pull them out from within the ashes and quickly removed the hot foil with his calloused hands. After they had cooled, he handed one to me whole: we ate our roasted potatoes plain, without butter, salt, chives, or sour cream. Frank chastised me with a teasing grin. "How can you be hungry in the middle of the afternoon? Doesn't your mother feed you?"

Frank liked to tease me, but somehow I always knew it was his way of helping me feel special. My parents didn't worry about me, a quarter of a mile down the street. I showed up as the afternoon wound down, well before it was time to set dinner plates on the table. And I was still hungry enough to eat that night's meal.

Our own acre of land was sandwiched between that of my grandparents and my uncle with unowned acreage between, on a street named for our family, maybe not much different than the early settlers who used their names to claim new streets and towns. Maybe someone would prevent us from continuing our independent neighborhood travels if we did something too terrible. Or as I learned later, if we thought something really bad happened nearby. Once Mom was terrified three years earlier when my just over one-year-old brother disappeared late one morning. I was too little to remember all of the details—with only sixteen months separating our births—creating a close and often competitive bond between us.

"Has anyone seen Mike? Michael! Michael!" she hollered after the last visitor departed down our gravel driveway following some meeting she'd been busy leading. Mom scurried through the kitchen, the living room, even looking in his crib. "Where is he?"

Brother Andy and I ran into the house to see what new incident had erupted this time. We set out to search. Finally, in fewer real minutes than worry minutes, Mom found Mike peacefully sound asleep next to a log at the beginning of the trail to Uncle Bill's house, his nearly white hair mussed and studded with the remains of maple tree helicopters. Drool dripped from his upturned mouth, long saliva strands reaching with the help of gravity to the dirt below. No worries seemed to peek through his slumber. Was this an early shout out to be noticed among this growing and boisterous clan? Or just the beginnings of the wanderings that we all continued?

Our excursions weren't always without our parents in tow. Occasionally, on an early fall Saturday we might load into our 1960s model station wagon and drive less than an hour from our quiet spot on the river into Northwest Portland, parking in the then-uncrowded dirt parking area of Macleay Park. We'd climb out of the car, following Dad's lead—our special tour guide who best knew the trails and secret places of this park and its larger adjacent wilderness gem, Forest Park. A park that today stretches for miles to create one of the largest urban reserves in the U.S. Dad is dressed in rugged Norm Thompson northwest attire of a plaid flannel shirt, softened by many washings, and his well-worn hiking oxfords.

Mcleay Park, 1969

"How far is it to the witch's castle?" we would ask him. An often-repeated question on this popular trek. We knew this was Dad's boyhood playground where he had built dams in the creek and forts in the brush with his brother Bill and neighborhood friends.

As we hiked along the trail, curving as it followed Balch Creek up into the hills, we stopped to catch our breath, and dawdled as we threw a few rocks into the rippled water. Two of us ran ahead, eager to be the first to get to our favorite part of the hike. It always seemed to be farther than we remembered. And then finally, after a final rise in the trail, the stone building stood before us.

"Did a witch really live here?" I asked.

Dad made a scary sound and a face. "Boo haha!" He laughed. Dad was at his finest with us, in the outdoors. He reminded us that this two-story stone building was all that remained of a ranger station and rest room built and quickly dismantled more than a decade ago. But every Portland kid I had ever known believed a witch once lived there. No roof remained, but a stairway led up into darkened corners that still seemed scary to me even if no witches lived here. We race up and down the stairs and I didn't want to be left upstairs by myself, but my older brothers, Pat and Andy, seemed unimpressed by any impending danger and laughed at my worries.

Most times we would keep hiking onward. As we got bigger and stronger, we might head toward the Pittock Mansion along our parents' favorite path, Wildwood Trail. The Pittock Mansion, originally the home of the founder of the Portland newspaper the *Oregonian*, even today boasts forty-six rooms and magnificent views of Portland below. Or we might select the path that headed in the opposite direction, Aspen Trail, with hopes of making it all the way to the bench at Inspiration Point. Mom, for much of her life, reminded us that this bench was our parents' favorite necking place. Dad instead told us about the Lonesome Fir, a slender spire jutting up in the midst of all this wilderness in full view at Inspiration Point. A coniferous tree that finally gave way to gravity, fading into the decomposing vegetation below when Dad was a teen.

The bench was also once a perfect viewing spot for Guild's Lake, the spot where Balch Creek meets the Willamette River. This seat of the local watershed became home to the 1905 Lewis and Clark Centennial Exposition on an artificially created island. This grand fair celebrated one hundred years after Lewis and Clark visited this part of the world. A fair that streamed lights and incited an aura of excitement to Dad's father, my grandfather Richard Gill Montgomery, Sr.—or more simply to us, Daddy Dick—as he watched as a child from the hills near his family's northwest Thurman Street home.

As we drove through this northwest Portland Willamette Heights neighborhood after our childhood hikes, and for decades after, my great-grandparents' original home was prominent near a stone drinking fountain in front on the sidewalk. The drinking fountain was first a horse trough early in the twentieth century, paid for by neighborhood kids who raised money after feeling sorry for the poor workhorses who had to climb the Thurman hill. My dad and his cousins remembered stuffing chestnuts into the dog dish section of the trough, but also found it a reliable water supply for squirting each other as kids in the 1930s. But on this 1960s venture, we drove past it and two other homes farther up Thurman to where Dad lived during his boyhood. As we slowly motored back down Thurman, we pulled over in our packed station wagon to look at the front porch of this most prominent home with the drinking fountain on the corner. Dad reminded us about all the Sunday mornings he and Bill would clamber down the hill from their house for waffles, cooked at the table by his grandmother, Georgia Gill Montgomery.

Dad with William and Georgia (Gill) Montgomery, Ann, Bill on 3115 NW Thurman Street, ca. 1936

I imagined looking out to the lights coming from the 1905 fair of yesterday: a time when our family and the earliest of white pioneers had already lived in this still wild and mostly undeveloped land for over half a century. A fair that tempted those from afar to recognize Portland as a real place, bringing in over a million and a half visitors, and encouraging newcomers who would double Portland's population in less than a decade. And after the fair was over, the land was dedicated to industry; industries unimaginable to fair attendees back then.

But it is within this park, that we strolled through so many times throughout the years with our dad, and he with his father and grandfather, like so many other Portlanders before and after, that lies Balch Creek. Its shallow waters that invited Dad to build dams, float pretend boats, and splash in the mud, begin in Portland's West Hills, and pick up momentum as it flows through a canyon abutting Cornell Road until it finally splashes through Forest Park's lowest section of Macleay Park. Finally, the creek enters a pipe and remains underground before tumbling into the Willamette River. Into a river that exudes memories of long-ago explorations and commerce; and stories of family told by Dad. A beloved river that magnetically drew Dad to the site where he built our home in 1964, immersing my brothers and I into our lives on the Willamette, creating a lifelong bond for us to this emerald jewel and launching us into this remarkable, often average, 1960s type of childhood.

CHAPTER 2
SNOW AND ICE

FALL LENGTHENS INTO winter; its penetrating dampness closes in. The musty, quiet river carries with it a sense of endings. Boat travel slows to a standstill. Fog and rain. The winter banks of the Willamette evoke memories of those who came before. When I was eight years old, I peered across the breadth of the Willamette in the heart of winter. Winter brought fog, rain, and—once in a while—snow.

Growing up in this not-yet incorporated land, I was starved for friends. Girlfriends. On this winter day, I imagined that if the river would ice over, I could walk across and just maybe meet a new girlfriend. The river never froze during our childhood. And I always wondered who lived across that muddy expanse in the house opposite ours, barely visible in the winter through the leafless cottonwoods. Out of view in the summer.

Had I known then, my snow-deprived self would have been jealous to have learned about the boisterous snowstorm that captured Portland and its surrounding areas just before Christmas in 1884. My great-great-grandfather, Joseph Kaye Gill—better known as J.K. and grandfather of our own Daddy Dick—penned in his diary how the snow continued for two days, falling so heavily that trains were blocked between The Dalles and Portland. And—as I stood on a lonely bank, wishing some eighty years later for the Willamette to freeze—the Columbia River had frozen over entirely. The Columbia River, the largest river in the Pacific Northwest: over twelve hundred miles in length, frozen. The river that begins in the Rocky Mountains of Canada's British Columbia, flowing northwest and then south into Washington state; turning west to form the border between Washington and Oregon before emptying into the grand Pacific Ocean.

Unlike my romantic imaginings so many years later during my childhood, blockaded trains full of men, women, and children began to exhaust their food supply.

"Food was hauled in on hand sleds from Hood River and Bonneville, (towns even then on the south side of Columbia) and then taken by men on foot to the trains. In this way the people were saved from starvation," J.K. scribed in his journal.

As people attempted to cross the ice, the powerful Columbia River Gorge wind blew so strongly that they couldn't stand up, and had to get down on hands and knees to cross. The wind that today delights wind surfers from all over the world must have felt like a terrible wrath sent down by the heavens above. When the trains finally got through to Portland, the volume of mail was so large it wouldn't fit inside the post office building—a post office then inside the oldest federal building in the Pacific Northwest: Portland's Pioneer Courthouse. A historic building today that opened in 1875 as the seat of government, holding then not just the post office, but courts, customs, and a tax office. And on that cold winter day, overflowing with mail. The storm reality of 1884 was a million miles away from my vision of sharing hot chocolate with a new friend in front of a warm fire.

As kids, every winter we always hoped for snows as deep as that. Like all kids in the milder longitudes of the Pacific coast, we would lie awake in bed praying that the few flakes we'd seen falling at bedtime would multiply overnight into deep powder drifts.

"Mike!" I would yell toward his adjoining bedroom. "Look outside! It looks white. It's snowing," I would cry, more excited than on Christmas morning.

"Do we have to go to school?" he asked.

Eagerly, almost painfully, we waited for some signal from Mom that school was cancelled. For it was Mom, always Mom, who helped us organize our days and made sure all meals got in our bellies. Patty Daum met Dad one college summer, working in a dentist office on Portland's west side—a job recommended by her Portland east side's Jefferson High career counselor. Dad was still attending to the expensive dental work begun after he knocked his teeth out playing football at Lincoln High. When he asked her out, Mom infamously told the handsome young man with the broken front teeth that she had a boyfriend, but to check back in six months. And that he did.

And as kids on those mornings when we actually got enough of that white stuff so that school was cancelled, as it might be a few days in our Willamette Valley each winter, Mom would share the message through our intercom. This newfangled intercom luxury

often broadcasted our parents' music selections to our bedrooms—
that was, when it worked. But this news about school being cancelled,
instead, delighted each of us kids in our warm beds. A bed that no
longer enticed us to dig deeper into its blanketed nest, unlike the
beckoning of an average school day.

Mike and Dede

We would hightail it through breakfast, often skipping it entirely,
to build our snow forts and snowmen and ambush each other with
wet packed snowballs: the usual wet snow of the Willamette Valley.
And off we would tromp over to my grandparents' house, perfectly
crafted with its sloping, grassy hillside dropping off at the riverbank.
Our grandmother, my namesake, Dorothy Haradon Montgomery—
WhoWho to us—would bundle up. She'd throw a blanket over her
shoulders, and look out at her grandchildren from the upper deck as
she sipped a cup of hot tea. Daddy Dick would step outside on the
deck as well, book in hand, and take the time to catch a couple puffs
of his pipe as he delivered his trademark hand wave. This day when
he wouldn't attempt his drive into Portland for work. When snow and

ice makes its appearance in the Willamette Valley, life as we normally know it stops. Daddy Dick's reading lamp just inside the living room, beyond the sliding double-glass doors, glowed through the fogged-up glass. But outside, the snow-covered hillside flowing down to the riverbank below was all a magical softness of snowy white.

This snowy day I jumped on our red flyer sled and it kept gliding—zipping down the snowy slope, catching speed as it neared the bottom, and on over the riverbank. The riverbanks of our homes were steep, especially during winter when the water runs lower, before snowmelts from the Cascade Range pour through in the spring. As I disappeared from view over the ridge of the bank, nobody watching held any real fear that I landed in the river.

"You faked that!" claimed my oldest brother, Pat, after I struggled to pull my sled back up the bank. "You could have jumped off before going over the bank!" he added.

My cousin Dennis smiled. Encouraging but wordless. He knew. I was a middle kid in a family of boys; simultaneously trying to figure out just how to be noticed and keep up with my brothers. I learned early that dangerous stunts sometimes seemed to be the ticket. As long as I wasn't breaking any rules.

Later that winter I read *Hans Brinker, or the Silver Skates*. Books: the basic food group of my childhood. In the deep of our Willamette Valley winter, more gray than white, I daydreamed about what a paradise it would be to live somewhere so cold that winters would invent frozen-solid rivers and canals. And about owning a pair of ice skates. My brothers and I had made the trek with our mom to Portland's Lloyd Center Ice Rink twice to try our skill at ice-skating. I hated it. Those early attempts to skate made my ankles ache, and my butt was bruised from falling. But reading about Hans Brinker, I envisioned I would be graceful, my hair flowing in the cool breeze as I gathered speed along the ice. I imagined icicles and sparkling crystals. Colorful wool knitted mittens and earmuffs. Now that would be something.

And one frosty day, it happened. The mud puddles from the day before had frozen solid in our gravel driveway.

"Hans!" I called. "I'm coming!"

I grabbed two plastic Franz Bakery bread bags from under the kitchen sink, put on my hand-me-down rain boots, black with the red stripe at the top, still a bit too large in the toe. I began my trek outside, down our driveway, which felt longer than a school day as a short-legged child. I crossed the road to our meadow: a meadow that lay lower than our own riverbank and separated our street, Montgomery Way, with the hill above where Wilsonville Road curved dangerously, decades before succumbing to straightening by an efficient road engineer. A meadow bisected by a creek in most seasons, surrounded by native grasses and invasions of scotch broom. A creek with stagnant pools where we caught polliwogs and salamanders. A meadow that decades later would be invaded by large, suburban homes.

That crystal day I hiked through the meadow, crunching through frosty grass. I crossed the bridge into River City, the imaginary, private waterfront resort of my oldest brother, Pat. River City appeared as a slightly higher rent district, neatly tended with a bridge constructed over the creek, efficiently created with leftover lumber from our new house: two beams with neatly nailed cross decking and a rope handrail. WhoWho and Daddy Dick liked to walk in our neighborhood and particularly enjoyed visiting this creek-side imaginary community, stopping to rest at the outlook jutting over the creek bank.

I barely remember how just a few years earlier, Pat had turned me into his real estate secretary-in-training, Mrs. Stake. Pat vaguely understood real estate, witnessing the selling of our Portland home to relocate to country living while I was just a baby.

Dede as Mrs. Stake, 1964

"DeDe, just sit here." He would motion to a small table and chair in my bedroom.

"Why?" I asked, a sometimes-adoring sister. The previous year I had responded by crying when a frustrated Pat threatened to leave me for good.

"Because I need your help. It's really easy," he explained.

"Why?" I repeated.

"Because you have to," he said.

"Why?"

"When I tell you to, just pick up your phone and say, 'How may I help you today?'"

"How long do I have to?" I asked.

"Just till we are done."

Shortly after I received my earlier telephone-etiquette career training, Pat and his younger-brother posse began projects with my dolls, one that required my mom to send my favorite, Sissy, to the doll hospital for a wig, after acts of scissor devastation—or was it imitating Portland Professional Wrestling? My other doll, a hand-me-down I named Steven, wasn't quite so lucky. There didn't seem to be any fix for Steven after early dismemberment operations severed all his fingers and toes and pushed his eyeballs into the back of his head, making him look like something straight out of a doll horror film. This all followed a special, non-parent-approved creation of my fourth birthday cake: a no-bake variety formulated by my older brothers. Chock-full of dog food with whipped cream topping. Most recently, Pat had sent me to Mars in a makeshift spaceship under a card table. It might have been exciting except for his space travel requirement that I first be blindfolded and led through complete darkness to be assaulted by prerecorded voices that amplified, burbling in a high-pitched tone: "We are going to eat you. We are going to eat you."

But on this winter day, after I crossed Pat's River City, I edged independently and unbothered by brothers into Andy's lower-rent district of Boone Borough—a somewhat unkempt property boasting a bridge entrance, if it could be called that. Andy, my spunky, always excited, gregarious brother, knew how to make friends and find adventure. In this case, the precarious crossing he crafted encouraged would-be trespassers to turn back or just wade across the stream rather than risk a collapse. But I was tiny and sure-footed, and I made it across the bridge.

Finally, I saw the ponds ahead! With the onslaught of our early Western Oregon winter rains, they were larger than I had ever remembered. A huge ice-skating rink! I thought. Stretching out in the distance from the direction I had come were our welcoming woods, stands of Douglas fir and spruce with a few maple trees lining the edges. Ahead of me, beyond the meadows, rose acres and acres of filbert and holly orchards. Now, finally, I would experience the freedom of gliding, just like Hans. I put the plastic bags over my too-big rain boots. I had even thought to bring rubber bands to secure the tops of the bread bags. I was ready: a moment of pure anticipation. I glided my right boot in what I imagined to be a graceful stride across the ice. I stretched out my arms and pictured all the twirls to come . . . as my boot caught an edge, and I clunked to a stop. Tragically, this pond, small and shallow, hadn't frozen in a smooth surface. It didn't invite any sort of gliding. Instead, my plastic-covered boots caught edges of grasses peeking through. Worse yet, the pond wasn't truly frozen solid and every few steps—not glides—my foot would break through the icy crust, disrupting any pretense of graceful skating.

I was heartbroken. Sadly, I trudged home. I wondered what it would be like to live in the Netherlands; or anywhere I could skate on a canal, a canal that would go on and on, an unbroken silver speedway.

Oh, what if I had known how our river lives would be disrupted—in just a handful of years, as I straddled teenage-hood—to a place of cold, snow, and ice. And how everyone but Dad would cry to leave the banks of our childhood.

CHAPTER 3
BASEBALL

IN THE WILLAMETTE Valley, our native *trillium* awakens us to spring. *Trillium ovatum*—otherwise known as wake-robin—springs forth even earlier than normal this year of 2016. We hope it's an anomaly, not a sign of things to come, even though we suspect differently as our summers continue to grow warmer and longer. Trillium can vary from white to purple, but always have the trademark collar of whorled leaves above a bare stem boasting a single flower with three petals, distinguishing it from any other. This flower spreads by rhizomes and if not disturbed can form large colonies, carpeting the woodland floor. Legend reminds us that picking parts of a trillium can harm the plant, as it stores much of its food in its leaves. Those special flowers we observe each spring can take up to seven years to grow on a new rhizome.

One spring afternoon when my own kids were young, I went to pick them up at day care. As I entered my five-year-old daughter's classroom, the teacher proudly announced, "Look what lovely spring flowers the children picked today."

I looked at the jar of ten single-stemmed, white-and-pinkish blooms. I turned to her aghast. Speechless.

"We walked across the street to Mary Young Park," she added. "The flowers were all over."

Mary S. Young Park: a vast natural haven bordering the Willamette River as it flows through the Portland southern suburban town of West Linn. A park boasting cottonwoods, maples, and Douglas fir. One of my family's favorite places.

"You didn't," I said, my voice louder than it should have been. Outraged.

"Why?" she asked.

My own daughter was now looking at me.

"You should know," I said, "it's illegal to pick this flower." Not sure that this was true, but comfortable using a commonly shared Oregon myth to make my point.

The teacher turned away to help other parents collect their kids. Unconcerned. I shook my head as I gathered my daughter and moved into the other room to collect her toddler sister. As we drove the short but steep distance home, I muttered disapproval for this teacher's lack of respect for our natural world. Of our own backyard.

"You girls know," I added, "that you shouldn't pick any kind of flower in a park, especially trillium, right?"

"Yes, Mom," they said in chorus,, beginning the early art of eye rolling. There was no mistaking, though. Teacher had done a very bad thing.

THE BLOSSOMS OF trilliums tease our souls into believing that sunshine is on its way, only to be chased by spring showers. But finally, spring bolts forth exuberant grasses and blossoming cherries. And the earliest smells of cottonwood. Unruly kids interrupt the classroom, yearning to be done with the school year. They anticipate time to be outside. To explore. A time for planting. And playing baseball.

In Wilsonville as in other small towns around the country, late spring meant baseball time. Little League in my day—no T-ball or year-round or girl teams yet for small kids who could barely throw a ball over the plate. I was introduced to most sports through my brothers, and baseball was no exception. When I was seven, conflict over a baseball led me to my first vocal accusation that Dad was a male chauvinist. We knew about women's lib as it was called in the 1960s. It took a few years before our dad caught on to how his only daughter would continue to stubbornly point out the steep learning curve ahead of him on issues related to women's rights. A job I took seriously. Though I eventually found some success, upon his retirement, Dad's female coworkers still referred to him as a "period piece." Dad liked to think this reference was due to his courtly manners, but in reality, there were some modern adjustments that were too challenging for him. He took a long time to accept replacing his black Olympia manual typewriter with his first computer. So long that his work colleagues created a plexiglass case for his cherished, left-behind writing instrument with the label, "Dick's Back Up Computer." And there was no doubt, as kind and gentle as my dad was, he struggled throughout his career to get up to speed up with the appropriate way to refer to women in the workplace.

One spring day—perhaps a bit like the first day of professional spring training—I cajoled Mike into playing catch with me in the yard, underneath our enormous, branching maple tree. Dad was in his bathroom, shaving with the window wide open, catching the fresh morning air. He looked out to see us tossing the baseball and impulsively yelled the phrase he would repeat in jest for another seven decades.

"DeDe! No hardball!"

Now honestly, how could he expect the only daughter of five children to respond?

"Dad!" I yelled. "That's not fair. What about Mike?"

Mike looked at me, a bit confused. What did he have to do with this conversation?

"You are a male chauvinist!" I added to Dad. I knew better than to add "pig" as Jane Fonda had popularized. I was starting to look for ways to question Dad. On this morning, Dad looked back at me, also a bit confused, half his face covered with shaving cream.

"Mike is younger than me. This isn't fair," I repeated. *What was the problem, exactly?* I wondered.

Silence still from Dad. He struggled with change—everything seemed to be happening so fast. But he was smart. "Both of you," he caught on. "You are both too young to play with the hardball. Use the softball." And he went back to his shaving.

Mike looked at me. "Thanks a lot," he mouthed.

The rule lasted about a day. And quickly Mike and I returned, without approval, to our usual game of catch. But for me it was a lesson. A lesson I learned I would be forced to repeat again and again.

Although I enjoyed playing catch with my siblings, when they weren't around or we got tired of each other, I spent hours in front of the pitchback rebound net my older brothers had received as a Christmas gift, perfecting my pitches. Actually perfecting my form—I don't think my accuracy was much to shout about. But I had two sharp-looking pitches, a stretch and a windup. I really thought the windup was more dramatic, dropping my right leg back, right hand with the baseball resting on the back of my right hip as I looked seriously to first the left, then the right at the imaginary base runners. I practiced throwing pitches over and over.

But I have to be honest. What I really coveted were the white flannel uniforms the boys who played Little League were assigned when they joined their teams. I was the most frequent loiterer at Mike's baseball practices, until finally, one season his coach asked me if I'd run bases. I was overjoyed. To be able to wear a batter's helmet. I excitedly ran the bases, outfitted still in my school clothes—a skirt, blouse, and scuffed, brown, buckled oxfords. As tired as I got, I was happy to keep trying to round those turns. Girls were not yet allowed to wear pants at Wilsonville Elementary, though it seemed so unfair when I learned that my Portland girl cousins were allowed to wear them every day if they wished. After a few times base running, I knocked the barely half-inch heel right off my right brown leather shoe. I had to glue it back on before I could wear them to school again.

It took a while, but finally, when I was eleven, our family's teenage friend, Jeff, offered to let me play on the Little League team he was coaching that summer. I didn't think much at first about being the only girl, although it was only 1972 and Tatum O'Neal and *The Bad News Bears* hadn't yet invited girls to imagine joining the ranks of boys' baseball, nor had the federal Little League charter yet been changed to allow girls to play. Few girls were breaking into Oregon Little League yet. But I was mostly excited about finally being able to wear the flannels of Little League.

I hadn't thought about being nervous, or even about it being a big deal. Until the first game day. I was so excited to put on my uniform, especially the knickers. There was something about knickers—they were just so cool, even if they were a little big on me. No cleats for us in those days, so I completed my outfit with a pair of tennis shoes. And then, suddenly it seemed, it was my turn at bat. I walked up to the plate, my hands rolling the grip of the wooden bat. Getting ready to choke up.

"That's a girl!" a dad in the bleachers yelled. My ponytail poked out from the back of my hat. "What's the girl doing out there! Get her off the field!" he added to the umpire.

Another dad joined in. His son was apparently the opposing pitcher, "Don't let that girl hit off you!" He made a scowling, mean face.

I turned and looked at Coach. *What's going on?* my expression asked. I played baseball with the boys at school all the time. I was better than most of them. Coach Jeff looked at me, his arms folded. He just shook his head. I stepped back to the plate and tried to ignore the shouting. Then I swung and hit the ball on the first pitch. I dropped the bat and ran as fast as I could. I rushed across first base, the shortstop fielder bobbling the ball before attempting an off-target toss to the first baseman. And those eleven- and twelve-year-old teammates of mine—unsure before about having a girl on their side—cheered loudly amid the taunts of their opposition. I rounded second on another base hit, crossed third on the next, and finally sprinted across home base, no slide needed.

I mouthed, "I told you so!" Glaring into the stands.

BASEBALL WAS MORE to us than just a popular American pastime. It was our dad's beloved sport, at least until he discovered handball. When I was a tot, Dad introduced me to my first uniformed teenaged baseball players when he coached a Babe Ruth team. I was thrilled to wear Pat's baseball hat backward on my head and watch the baseball players. We held baseball games at our annual Fourth of July party on the banks of the river, with our parents' friends from high school and college, and their families. We played at the beach where Dad demonstrated his "Sal Isaac batter stance" named after a Portland Beavers catcher with a lot of heart but not much talent who dribbled hits to the infield. He'd follow that up with "John Everything," a powerhouse natural hitter, as Dad pushed out pop flies over our beach house. Our dad grew up playing baseball, at one point in high school, wearing the uniform of Portland's Lincoln Cardinals, though he claims his hot start diminished by the time he was a high school senior, with a great arm and a lousy bat.

Dad batting at Wallace Park, 1945

Dad's first home, 3306 NW Thurman, 1938

Dad's finest baseball memories were created at Portland's Vaughn Street Park, in the flatlands just below Forest Park and Balch Creek near the original Guild's Lake. The echoing of "play baaaallll!" of decades past lives on still in this neighborhood, home of the Lucky Beaver Stadium. Built in 1901, Lucky Beaver was home to the Portland Beavers, followed by other teams until 1956, holding out as one of the last remnants of Portland's original Slabtown neighborhood. The original Slabtown nickname came from the lumber mills in the area, selling "slabs" as a cheap heat source in this working-class neighborhood that was then home to marginalized groups of Portlanders. Most memorable to Dad of all things baseball: his scoreboard job at this stadium. The excitement of the games, with thousands of Portlanders flocking by streetcar and foot to the Lucky Beaver: Dad's home away from home.

For Dad and other Portland boys like him growing up in the 1930s, the ballpark was ruled by its Model-T–driving groundskeeper-king, Rocky Benevento, a man (some say) so popular he could have been elected mayor. Benevento kept Slabtown's potential young troublemakers off the streets by hiring them to keep Vaughn Street green, clean, and beautiful. Dad learned early on how to be valuable to this local hero, shagging foul balls hit outside the park and promptly returning them to the stadium management.

Dad coveted the score keeping job at Lucky Beaver Stadium, hoping he might have a shot at working the scoreboard. And he got it! Dad shared the job with a set of classmates, twin brothers, John and Jim. It was a two-person job, but Rocky figured, no separate identity for the twins: they could share the job. Dad and the twins earned $5 per game and $7.50 for a doubleheader. They'd climb a rickety ladder up to the scoreboard, perched high above the center field bleachers, the ladder trembling during gusty winds as they reached to set the tin plates identifying runs. Before the first pitch could be delivered, these lucky boys also climbed the ladder to raise the American flag.

"Oh say can you see, by the . . ." Seeing his son raise the flag during our national anthem—even on a rickety ladder—most pleased his father, our Daddy Dick. At this time, Dad was growing into a full-fledged fear of heights: later on, my brothers would push the envelope, teasing Dad by feigning falls from cliffs, dams, and canyons. But somehow, the excitement within the ballpark masked his fear.

The scoreboard in those days had no contact with the public address announcer, so the young scorekeepers watched the umpire like hawks to keep the balls and strikes up on the scoreboard. When they missed, the announcer would quietly correct them: "Ahem, that is two strikes, folks, not one." Briefly embarrassed, the kids would correct their mistake as cheers echoed through the Lucky Beaver.

Dad moved on from this job, but working the scoreboard always held the blue-ribbon spot in his heart. And fifty-nine years later, in 1991, Dad received an unexpected extra inning. He and the Holt twins, now senior citizens with creaking knees and slower steps, were invited to climb up a seventy-foot ladder—now equipped with guardrails—to the scoreboard at the then-new PGE Park. The home team, who played at PGE Park for a short while until the park was modified to be a soccer- and football-only stadium, was once again called the Portland Beavers and the hits were recorded on a vintage hand-operated scoreboard. Wearing headphones, the three original Lucky Beaver scorers directed a new generation of rookie scorekeepers.

I ALSO STRUCK out during my first Little League season, and I no longer remember how many hits I got or errors I made. But I can still feel those flannels on my eleven-year-old skin. And hear the crack of that first hit. And though I was heading into an era of indifference toward Dad, I am sure now of just how proud he was to see me on the field. His only daughter—the only girl he ever watched on the field playing Little League—in baseball flannels in the summer of 1972.

CHAPTER 4
SUMMER

SUMMER IS TRUE river time. Lazy summer emanates nature's special recipe: a potpourri of carp and cottonwood that transports any grown-up river kid back to childhood on the rivers of the Willamette Valley. After cottonwoods cover banks and nearby roads with white fluffy fibers, mowers and tractors hew lawns and till soil. The milky fibers drop from overhanging limbs into the Willamette, creating a strangely enticing scum. The smell of river summer doesn't fully ripen until late June. It rises mildly on a morning, simmering until late afternoon as the banks absorb the sun's warmth and then, finally, release the ultimate summer river smell: a fishy blend spiked with decomposing cottonwood fibers and soon-to-burst blackberry blossoms.

For river kids, after chores and work shifts were finished, summer meant long, lazy days and evenings to swim and—if lucky—ride in a boat. We shook with excitement to cruise the river in a ski boat, a canoe, or even a leaking rowboat—simultaneously trolling for crawdads while dumping water overboard as it accumulated in the middle of the boat bottom. Oh, and who could forget how delicious that river water felt on a hot summer day?

During the midafternoon hours we pieced together as many minutes as we could gather for river time. My brothers and I dashed down from the house to the ramp—its runged height changing to match river levels. Running, jumping off the dock, stretching our limbs like Olympian long jumpers as we leapt out into the current as far as our human springs allowed. The cool water hit us, first kissing our toes, striking through our cores, and finally engulfing our scalps as we sank ten feet under: a silent moment, down below, before we rose in gloriousness to the cottonwood-smelling, warmer surface. This water that renewed our dusty, sweaty bodies: treaded water, dipped under, and treaded again.

"There's a warm spot here!" one of us would yell.

Willamette River at Wilsonville, 1969

Our bodies were living thermometers, measuring temperature differentials between depths.

We climbed up on the dock, shivering and claiming the best hot, dry spots to stretch out on our stomachs. Our bodies dried luxuriously; our skin tickled. We inched to a new dry spot, until at last we radiated heat. We jumped up and dashed to the dock edge to cannonball into the water, crashing through reflections of trees from the bank and clouds above. Rinse and repeat. Next time we tossed out an inner tube and hoped the wind and current didn't move it too fast down the river before we could jump and reclaim it. We pulled our arms through the water, kicked our legs—and paused to squint upriver. We hoped to spy an approaching tugboat and barge to create a wake for our favorite river dance: up and down, as the river flowed. Until, finally, the sun dropped lower in the sky and our bellies grumbled a warning that dinnertime was near.

WE KIDS DIDN'T know then that as we nudged into the 1970s, we sat at an intersection of land development in Oregon. Our state was on the brink of disputing the false early Oregon legend that our fertile Willamette Valley land would be forever green and abundant. Newly elected Oregon visionaries exposed the truth: our land could not be developed without bounds and still maintain its glory.

Was it the influence of growing up during Governor Tom McCall's reign that so profoundly affected us, unlocking our passion to care so much about the river, its valley and history? In 1962, Tom McCall, a graduate of the University of Oregon's Journalism School like our dad, produced *Pollution in Paradise* prior to his reign as governor while he was a reporter with KGW television. A documentary that is cited, even today, as it informs younger generations and transplants and those who may not have been listening before about our past and future. Upon his election, our governor, preceding even environmental regulations, fought to restore health to the Willamette and tried to teach us about what we could lose.

"Hello, Monty!" Tom McCall would call later to my dad or to Daddy Dick when they occasionally encountered each other. Tom was an old friend of my dad and his father from earlier days when the KGW account was held by the Montgomery Advertising Agency, which Daddy Dick owned and where Dad worked in those early years creating copy alongside his brother Bill.

And then Oregonians began to talk about pollution. Our Willamette—some days loaded with effluent—touting sludge hazards awaiting would-be swimmers. The nearby town of Tualatin, known to us for its annual Crawfish Festival, was forced to stop developing until it created a sewer system to prevent the Tualatin River from becoming a permanent cesspool. It might have been an early edition of *Life* magazine that tainted Dad's interest in living on the Tualatin River after its pages designated it as one of the most polluted waterways in America. The most noticeable culprit in the 1960s was effluent: the leaching chromium from old tanneries invisible to the eye and not targeted by federal government superfund cleanup until several decades later. The town of Tualatin with its primary industry after its sawmill and brickyard had closed up decades before—Blue Mountain Pet Food that sported its slogan "Going to the Dogs" on its delivery trucks. And it was Tualatin, thanks to Governor McCall, a federal grant, and the Oregon-based engineering company CH2M Hill, that by the end of the 1960s had built the country's second state-of-the-art tertiary-level sewage treatment facility, following the lead of Las Vegas.

Andy and Dede, United Sewerage ad, ca. 1969

But what I knew then was that I had to pose holding hands with Andy with our backs to the camera while we stood on our dock, sadly looking at our sometimes effluent-encumbered river. I remember thinking it odd when Dad shot the picture, with us looking so sadly down into a river that was at least on that day clean enough for swimming. Or, perhaps, at least I thought it was. Me with my mismatched knee socks missing elastic and collared shirt messily tucked into my school skirt. I would never meet model specifications. But Dad, prolific with kids, didn't need real models as he created advertising copy to promote cleaner, healthier rivers for Oregonians. And under McCall's administration, Oregon became a model for effluent treatment facilities as our municipalities sought to comply with the then-new 1972 Clean Water Act. Our rivers became swimmable again. It wasn't until several decades later that the lower Willamette's Portland Harbor sediments and bottom-dwelling fish were found to contain toxic concentrations of heavy metals, polychlorinated biphenyls and pesticides: contaminants that required expensive and sophisticated analysis, regulations, and cleanup. All remnants from a century of industrial chemical use along our beloved waterway.

SUMMER NIGHTS ALONG the riverbanks in our Willamette Valley serve cool breezes laden with an aftertaste of blackberries, and accompanied by a cricket symphony.

When it got dark, we went walking. It started simply: Mom went out by herself, starved for peace and solitude in our boisterous household. And then, one night, she invited us. We walked along our lane—quiet but for the sounds of frogs and crickets. If we were really silent, we might hear an owl. And then, one night, for reasons only understood by those who still believe in magic, we began hiding from cars: diving under the scratchy limbs bearing fading yellow scotch broom blossoms, or behind the birch trees if we were lucky enough to be near them, whenever a light-and-noise-blaring monster of the night sped past. And Mom hid too! Sometimes if we couldn't find any other suitable hiding place, we just dove down in the tall grasses sticking up along the side of the road, hoping to be miraculously hidden. No sidewalks for us country folk; very few houses graced our lane with none of them close together. Surprisingly, even on our quiet road, cars did come along—though not often enough to satisfy our cravings for the nervous anticipation and rapid heart-beating, the self-inflicted fear, they provoked.

"No, Mike. I'm back here! Shh. Quick. Hurry! One is coming!"

No extra lights in the sky: advancing headlights morphed into powerful spotlights as cars turned off the main road to our quiet lane. We dashed to a hiding place. Hearts pounding, imagining what might happen should we be spotted. Maybe we would be chased.

"Shh! No whispering!" This was when we knew. We knew that our mom was fun. And an adventurer. One of us.

EVERY NIGHT IN our riverside home, Mom came to each of us alone in our beds at our prescribed bedtime for "talk time." A time to be savored in a family with five kids. We talked about our day and often said our prayers together. I felt loved and safe. But after she left, on those weeknights when Dad wasn't at home, I awaited the sound of car tires traveling up our gravel driveway just outside my bedroom window. And then I would hear loud voices. Arguing. And the slam of the door. The sound that I knew—as I got old enough to sense the conflict—was Mom heading out for a walk. Dad did most of his heavy drinking late nights after work and not around the house, leaving him sober on weekends during our family times together outdoors and on the river. But I began to identify beer at its lowest odor threshold. And, ever so slowly—the older I got—I grew intolerant of it, and of our dad.

BUT OUR DAYS were glorious. Back then, we rode our bikes confidently and freely on our little lane—especially in the summer. Each red Schwinn was passed down from one sibling to the next as our legs grew too long for the frame: always boy-framed bikes with a middle bar. Though an occasional cause of emergency room visits, those red bikes magnified our ability to explore. Bikes: a universal first freedom. We kept to our quiet lane until brave enough to handle the traffic and narrow shoulders of Wilsonville Road's trademarked S curves. We tirelessly challenged ourselves to break our individual records of rounding the turnaround at the far end of the lane without hands: a dozen circles completed without touching the handlebars. A turnaround at the edge of our woods, far away from any through traffic.

"I counted thirteen!" I'd yell proudly, my knees skinned from earlier trials. And one scar.

Occasionally, Mom would jump on a bike and join us kids. But never Dad—not in those years. Dad had grown up riding a bike: it was by bike that he completed the early morning rounds of his first newspaper job, delivering the *Oregonian* to his Northwest Portland neighbors. And it was by bike that Dad learned, during one early morning delivery, how poorly brakes work on racing wheels in Willamette Heights' steep hills, crashing into pavement and breaking his nose for the first time. Dad didn't venture to ride a bicycle again until he turned seventy-two—long after our glory days in Wilsonville had fled. This time around, Dad, a man of routine, only reluctantly agreed to pedal again to keep up with his wife: we'd given Mom a bike for a birthday gift, and she was revving up. Dad insisted he would only join Portland's bike frenzy if he could find a model similar to his childhood model Schwinn—never one to want the latest and greatest. He compromised on a yellow-and-black Giant three-speed.

Impulsive and animated, Dad immediately became an enthusiastic senior member of Portland's avid biking community, especially on not-too-hot sunny days. Dad hated the heat. He liked best to pedal away from his river-view Sellwood neighborhood condo, his home of twenty late-life years and the last Portland neighborhood in which he would reside. He would ride along the Springwater Corridor and the Willamette River Esplanade, past the statue of his friend Mayor Vera Katz, across the Steel Bridge and the Willamette River. He rode to his post-retirement gigs, never interested in completely retiring, and he rode to meetings at the Oregon Maritime Museum—the steamer moored at Tom McCall Waterfront Park in downtown Portland, resurrected during his tenure as the museum's president. Dad pedaled to the Alcoholics Anonymous meetings that helped him become the old man he was, in his old stomping grounds of Northwest Portland. And once, for reasons he didn't know at the time, he fainted while riding on a sidewalk on Northwest 23rd Avenue. Dad didn't carry a cell phone, neither did he want to bother anyone, so he picked himself up after hitting a parked car, and rode on home with blood dripping down his leg. Other days he and Mom bicycled together and reminisced about old Portland over cups of coffee in the newly fancy and expensive Northwest Pearl District. Enjoying their days. Not yet imagining a time when one of them might be left without the other.

Even as an old man, Dad was unmistakable: those muscled calves pedaling, a thick shock of white hair poking out from his helmet, and secret river memories flooding his pores. At eighty, after falling a couple of times, he permanently parked the yellow-and-black cruiser in a corner of his garage. Air slowly seeped out of the tires of his Giant, but Dad was never one to regret. Still, he pedaled in place: cottonwoods in his mind, music in his ears.

CHAPTER 5
HEART STRINGS

AS KIDS IN Wilsonville, some mornings we were awakened by measures of the *Grand Canyon Suite* or a chorus of "Hello, Dolly!" pumping through the main living area of our house by record player. The 1960s intercom system that played into each of our rooms amplified our parents' favorite classical radio station and allowed our parents to broadcast their own personal message to us. Each bedroom in our house on the Willamette was equipped with a satellite unit with just a Push to Talk switch and a volume control. Back then, I imagined how rich we must be to have such a system, though it really didn't work much of the time. Throughout our communal downstairs, we would listen to our parents' collection of classical symphonies and musicals on the record player—later our parents' almost touching on hipness as they discovered Burt Bacharach, Herb Alpert, and the Carpenters. Us kids were introduced to Burt Bacharach well before we saw the 1969 *Butch Cassidy and the Sundance Kid*—destined to become our favorite movie—laced with the songs of Bacharach. After seeing *Butch Cassidy* on the big screen, we watched it repeatedly, religiously, years later on late-night TV. Dad liked to announce how he had a love affair with Paul Newman and Robert Redford as they played bad-boy Western outlaws. Each movie scene was imprinted in my brothers' minds to be reenacted later as shoot-outs on the beach and cliff jumps in the nearby woods. And our dad, who could be such a ham, might occasionally be found singing phrases of "Raindrops Keep Falling on my Head" in the hallways of our home.

MICHAEL RECENTLY CONFIDED that he, like me, once had great hopes of becoming famous. While I considered Broadway, Michael dreamed of becoming a singer. I only just heard this solemn confession as a pianist played "Raindrops Keep Falling on my Head" on Mother's Day at the assisted living facility where Mom lives now.

As we listened, surrounded by many more elderly women than men, Michael sheepishly described how he would sing this song aloud as he walked along Montgomery Way to our bus stop perched at the top of the steep Rose Lane hill. He sang the song over and over, proudly admiring his voice. First making sure nobody else was within earshot. For days in a row at age eight, he perfected his performance. Decades before *American Idol*, brother Mike set his sights on big things.

One fortuitous day, a classmate left a tape recorder on the bus home from school. Mike knew this was his chance: he rescued the tape recorder from its abandonment in the corner of the dark green bus seat, leaving behind its sad partner—a lonely, forgotten lunch box, probably filled with sandwich crusts. Once off the bus, Mike sang the song, over and over, pacing the many steps to our house. Practicing. Getting ready for his debut. Finally, he was alone, next to the grand maple tree in our yard. This was his opportunity to critique his voice, to forge ahead toward his new path of stardom! Nervously, he pulled every ounce of his melodic strength together, concentrating to record his best effort ever, watching the tape as it wound from one cassette reel to the other. He manually rewound the tape and sat down, palms sweating, as he turned the recorder switch to Play. And he couldn't believe it. This wasn't the voice he heard as he walked down Montgomery Lane, focused and unaware of the holly orchard and birch trees he passed.

This is an imposter! he thought. He had never heard his voice through others' ears before.

Shoulders slumped. Tennis shoes dragging. Glumly, he carried the recorder and his own lunch box into the house. He dropped them on the floor inside the back door. A sad night awaited him. Quiet through dinner. Nighttime dreams of a brightly lit stage, dashed upon the morning's reminder. As he climbed on the bus that day, Mike reluctantly set the tape recorder back in the cardboard box of forgotten things next to our bus driver, Cap. A box for all things abandoned. He was crushed. At eight, his singing career was over.

Unlike my brother, Broadway musicals were my entrancement. Oh—to be on stage! I, too, imagined being discovered. I sang my favorite songs repeatedly, my brain imprinted with lyrics to every musical popular during the twentieth century. The musicals my parents played over and over on our family record player. *The Sound of Music. My Fair Lady. Doctor Doolittle. Show Boat. Carousel. Camelot.*

Oklahoma! Disappointedly, so far, my only solo had been in Mrs. Rigall's third-grade Wilsonville class. Mrs. Rigall seemed to like quiet girls a lot more than the other kids, and had a small silver bell on her desk she rang to get our attention. She had written an original play, oddly, about wind. Each of us students was assigned a unique wind to act out in a costume designed and sewn by each of our mothers or sisters or grandmas. Maybe even an undisclosed father. The wind that spoke to me—that I yearned to be assigned—was a breathless, beauty wind. Pink! Heartbreakingly, this wind was assigned, in the end, to Mary Lou—the girl with the most beautiful voice in our class. The same girl who had been assigned the solo in our class song, "The Little Drummer Boy," performed at the Christmas concert. Mrs. Rigall assured us, as she assigned roles, that each would receive an equal and fine part. No tryouts for us. I was crushed to hear the role I was assigned: the Dopey Wind, with predictably disappointing lyrics.

"They call me a dopey wind. Sometimes I blow fast, then slow, but sometimes I don't know where to go. So yes, I am a dopey wind. So what if I'm not so smart. But I'm really a good wind at heart."

The lyrics made me feel so sad. I just felt sure there had to be more in store for me than singing about not knowing where to go, costumed in a pale blue wrap.

Not long after, a local college theater department advertised an upcoming production of *Fiddler on the Roof.* I was so excited and begged Mom to let us attend. I had been spending hours singing "Matchmaker," fully choreographing how I would sway and pose as I sang, borrowing an apron from the kitchen as I, too, worked in secret to perfect my voice. My sway. Expressions of yearning and hope for my imagined audience. The night of the show I was so excited—I had seen only a few live theater productions. The children's theater in our day, the Portland Zoo's Ladybug Theater, stuck to fairy tales, and once when we went there on my birthday, my brothers threatened to volunteer me to the oven during a production of *Hansel and Gretel.*

Back then, it was very unusual for our parents to shell out money for tickets to live productions in downtown Portland: *Hello, Dolly!* was an early exception. When in an especially good mood, Dad would prance around and sing the first few lines of its theme song to me. "Helloooooo, Dolly," he'd sing. Hamming it up to the point where, as I got older, I would roll my eyes and walk away. As a teenager, sadly, I lost my tolerance for his overzealous expression.

The appointed date for the big night at the college theater, I put on my best school dress. I excitedly read the program as we waited in the semi-darkened theater. That's when it happened: the moment of betrayal. My friend Kelly's name was listed as one of Tevye's daughters. I couldn't believe it. I felt duped. Why had I not been told about this opportunity? After all the practicing I had done. Did they not know that I, too, was the perfect age and size? Yes, Kelly had red hair—but I, too, could look Eastern European. I could be Jewish, I thought. I sat spellbound in the audience—so sad now as I awaited the opening scene. At last, the overture began and I was transfixed to witness in person the music I'd only heard floating from a record player. And when, finally, Kelly came onstage, I had to admit she was good and cute and fit in with the rest of the cast. But still I felt left out. As if I had missed my opportunity.

The next year my parents took us to a local theater production of *Oliver!* We knew both the movie and soundtrack by heart.

"You want more?" Dad would ask, over and over, in the tone of Bumble speaking to a trembling Oliver. Dad would say the word *more* a half octave higher, and he would open his eyes wide, giving them a disturbing, slightly scary look. Dad treated this line as a sort of all-purpose phrase; I rolled my eyes.

The songs, however, were my favorite, and I knew all of them. "Wheeeeeeeeeeeere is Love?" I'd croon, complete with the winsome, troubled look of Mark Lester, the young actor in the original movie—though I was later traumatized to learn his songs were dubbed by a girl. I would try to find cast-off clothing in my brothers' drawers to help complete my orphan aura. I knew I had perfected this song. Again, I was so excited to be in the audience, this time at Portland's Civic Theatre, I eagerly pored over the program. I read the name of the actor cast as Oliver. And again! I couldn't believe it.

"There is a girl playing Oliver!" I whispered to Mom. I looked at her—my eyes questioning loudly. *How could this be*, I wondered? *I could have had a shot at this part, too.* I had never considered that a girl would be allowed to play the part of a well-known boy's role. Troubled, I listened as the show started with the music that had played over and over in our home. But, as with *Fiddler on the Roof*, the joy of being at the theater won over: as I listened to the music, transfixed by the dark and depressing sets of London, the magic outshone my discontent, and I mouthed along with every word.

LATER, I MADE my appearance in school shows. The only musical was an eighth-grade performance of *Snow White*. I did enjoy the attention I received singing solos about a prince, even if it was terribly embarrassing to have my first kiss ever from a boy onstage in front of people. I didn't want to admit I had never before kissed a boy: I practiced my skill before opening night, alone with my wrist. And then, finally, with the boy named John in our dress rehearsal: the prince of our play.

"Do it like you mean it," John whispered to me after our first attempt on stage. With a weak smile and red cheeks—I just knew he was more experienced than me—we prepared to try again as Mrs. Schuster had us repeat the scene.

"That was better," John told me, trying to be helpful.

During my big song, singing about my prince coming someday, I almost hit the high notes, reaching into a weak falsetto on "moment" and "dreams."

Dad teased me about this performance—kindly—for the remainder of his days. "I really liked how you handed out those sack lunches to those dwarves," he'd say, over and over. "You were so good at that," he added with a teasing smile. Not until my twenties did I truly smile back at this joke. But even at the time, there was no doubt in my mind: this show held no candle to *Fiddler on the Roof* or *Oliver!*, the real musicals we listened to in our house on the banks of the river.

RIVER MUSIC. BABBLES and bubbling, gurgles and splashes. Gentle lapping of the current as it nudges the docks and sandy banks. Crashing symphonies as winter winds create ocean-like waves and shriek through the bare cottonwood branches. Wakeful spring: morning flights of heron rustling bursting leaves. Lullabies of hushed winters, dripping springs. Infusing our lives with the river.

Back in my earliest river days on the Willamette, we would wander the eighth of a mile to our grandparents' home, *Riverbank*. Classical violin sonatas or the melodies of the Irish would be streaming out the front door. This home was the highlight of their life together, until age and illness forced them back into urban Portland. Built in 1963, it initiated our own move, from the house in the city where I was born to the banks of the Willamette in Wilsonville. Daddy Dick, the great-grandson of Chloe Clark and William Willson—who together traversed this river during times of canoes and steamboats over a century earlier, boating on the river outside our back door between Salem and the Willamette Falls. And WhoWho, who raised sheep, bumper lambs, geese, chickens, poodles, and Airedales. This was their dream home, made even sweeter by both of their sons' families living nearby.

I escaped daily to visit with my special grandmother who listened to my stories and rescued me from an overwhelming sea of boys.

"How about a nice cup of tea?" she would ask me. I would nod as I watched her put on the teakettle. WhoWho taught me how to make cambric or "children's tea," as she dipped an English Breakfast tea bag briefly into a china cup of just-boiled water. Her blue willow dishes were my favorite, a reminder for me of the book *Blue Willow*. The tea, now with a hint of brown, she would whiten with milk and sweeten with sugar.

"Sit thee down," she would say. WhoWho gave me her full attention.

As my brothers and I crossed the threshold of *Riverbank*, music would stream from either our grandfather's den or the living room. When Pat stopped by with his viola, Daddy Dick would take it by the grip, go into the living room with its plate glass windows looking out over the Willamette, and play the viola like a cello. The cello: our grandfather's instrument, from his beginnings in Portland's Lincoln High Orchestra to later performances in Portland recital halls.

"DADDY DICK, WILL you go to my orchestra concert tomorrow night?" Patrick asks.

"Wouldn't miss it, Pat-the-Wat," our grandfather replied, who coined nicknames for each of us and inspired brothers Pat and Andy to carry the creation of nicknames, many much cruder, onward to future generations. Thanks to my brothers, during my childhood I became Dorkus, Dumdum, and Doodoo.

The next night, our family filed into the West Linn High School gym, joining other families from across the school district for this concert, a district mixing kids from then-unincorporated Wilsonville with those of West Linn. Parents and grandparents: proud of their children learning strings. Younger siblings hanging on, holding out, hoping maybe they would get a special dessert later if they could just make it through the long evening without incident. The Wilsonville contingent was mostly represented by farming families. Our Daddy Dick sat among them like a refined English country gentleman, wearing a collared shirt and sport jacket, perched on a well-worn, creaky upper bleacher overlooking the high school basketball court.

The kids in the spotlight were dressed up in their Sunday best: Pat proudly wore a sport coat with slightly mismatched slacks usually reserved for church; scuffed shoes. The music began—squeaks and off-tune strummings and squawkings of new musicians. It didn't matter. The English gentleman fixed his eyes on his grandson. His hands moved to mimic holding a bow, moving it back and forth in beat with the hands of the eleven-year-old string players. He swayed to the music, never moving his eyes from his grandson on the floor of the gymnasium—for now, elegant as any recital hall.

"That was grand," he whispered in Patrick's ear afterward.

A NUMBER OF years later, after several seasons of renting a basic student model from Wally's Music Shop in Oregon City, Daddy Dick and WhoWho surprised me with a silver Armstrong flute for my thirteenth birthday. A shockingly more expensive gift than they had ever given me. A gift intentionally selected to mark my move into teenage-hood.

"Do you prefer being called a flutist or a flautist?" Daddy Dick would ask. Not joking. He was very interested. Always quietly interested. He must have been secretly pleased when I moved past shrill squeals of passages of "A Simple Gift" to classical selections of Bach and Telemann. He passed before I discovered sheet music to play his favorite jigs: those of the Irish.

Music came to Daddy Dick from his parents, my great-grandparents, who were active participants in early Portland Opera. Daddy Dick's father, William Andrew Montgomery, must have introduced his wife—Daddy Dick's mother—Georgia Gill Montgomery, to opera. I suspect Georgia's upbringing had mostly exposed her to Methodist devotional music. Early Portland Opera performances beginning in the late 1800s drew audiences to the Marquam Building's fifteen-hundred seat Orpheum Theater—a theater that also went by other names through the years; Hippodrome and Marquam Grand Opera

House. A theater that even hosted authors all these years ago: Mark Twain drew a standing-room-only crowd in 1895. The Marquam Building eventually collapsed under the weight of its brick in 1912. The theater moved to temporary locations, and the spot developed into the American Bank Building: what we know today opposite downtown Portland's Pioneer Square.

William Montgomery (right) opera, 1898

My great-grandfather William Andrew Montgomery had a most beautiful voice, and although he dabbled in opera, he was a founder and longtime member of the Apollo Club, a Portland men's singing club. He also was an officer in the 1917 Portland Music Festival. This festival showcased a chorus of 250 voices and the Portland Symphony Orchestra to dedicate the new public auditorium, with profits from the event supporting the war relief effort. The auditorium: the same stage all Portland public high school graduates like me walked across to accept our high school diplomas sixty-some years later in the late 1970s. The same auditorium—though remodeled as today's Keller Auditorium—where I'd sit front-row with my own daughters, two decades after my own graduation, watching a production of *Annie.*

"MOMMY! REMEMBER WHEN I was on this stage?" Emily had whispered to me before the orchestra began the overture in this modern-day auditorium that swallowed small children into its darkened hollows. She smiled and wiggled in anticipation of the show, delighted that I had forked out entirely too much money for front row seats.

I was relieved as I looked at my youngest daughter—she needed no reminders about proper theater etiquette. I smiled at the memory of her onstage just two years prior as one of a handful of kids donning blonde wigs and white wings to play impish angels in Portland Opera's first international collaboration of *La Belle Hélène* in 2001. Set on this same stage. Capitalizing on opportunities for kids that I had merely dreamed about.

FOR CHLOE CLARKE—Georgia Gill Montgomery's grandmother; my great-great-great-grandmother; Emily's great-great-great-great-grandmother—music provided a simple but serious pleasure on her arduous journey aboard the *Lausanne*. At twenty-one years old, Chloe left her hometown of East Windsor, Connecticut to join the Jason Lee missionary expedition of 1839: sailing around the horn of South America to reach the Oregon Territory. This, a religious mission "to save the souls of Indians."

Chloe carried few possessions. Her seaward journey was easier than walking or riding the many tough miles of the Oregon Trail, yet still nearly incomprehensible to most modern travelers. Chloe was confined to the *Lausanne* for nine months, unsure whether she would ever see family again. As waves tossed the ship up and down, passengers struggled with relentless seasickness. A self-proclaimed Christian and devout believer, Chloe wrote in her journal as she attempted to attain true devotion to her God.

"I find that situated as we are in our small rooms and many of us sick and almost everything unlike what we have been used to having we have need of great patience and have a fine opportunity for cultivating that grace."

When she crossed the equator on a November day in 1839, Chloe wrote of her daily routine: "filling every moment of the day to avoid any empty time to complain or repine." While others on the boat journaled about stopping over in South America's Rio de Janeiro after sixty-five days onboard and observing veiled women, or later rejoicing in the surfacing of whales, Chloe writes about her commitment to God. Though most of her time was dedicated to prayer meetings, Chloe squeezed an hour of music study into each day and, twice a week, time for singing schools. Chloe played her melodeon—an early organ relying on free reeds but no pipes, foot pedals to work its bellows and carried it with her to soothe the travel- and sea-weary, and to praise God for safe travel on the long journey westward. And unlike those who would a few years later toil on the Oregon Trail and carry melodeons, mixing the reeds with the notes of fiddles, harmonicas, and flutes to create reels and jigs and tunes like "Old Joe Clark," Chloe sang devotions to God.

Chloe Clarke Willson

WHILE CHLOE CLARKE and my great-great-grandfather, J.K. Gill, were filled with English blood and early American Methodism, the musical taste of Daddy Dick—through his father with the beautiful voice, William Andrew Montgomery—was spiced with love of the Irish. Daddy Dick was eager to share the Irish heritage that came to us from William's parents, who emigrated from Enniskillen, Ireland, during the Potato Famine first into Canada, and finally New England. The music closest to Daddy Dick's heart was music of the Irish.

In 1974, as he neared the end of his life, Daddy Dick donated his entire Irish tenor John McCormack vinyl collection to Portland's Multnomah County Library. To some, John McCormack was the most popular of all Irish singers and sometimes said to be as popular in the United States in the 1920s as Elvis Presley was in the 1950s. Daddy Dick's collection was one of the largest McCormack collections in the world: accumulated over twenty-five years and containing all the discs the tenor made, from his first efforts to his final recordings in 1942: a collection containing nearly six hundred songs and arias. Daddy Dick had labeled each of his 78 rpm records with a British flag for those purchased in England, a shamrock for the discs from the Emerald Isle, and without a designation if purchased in the US. This collection was Daddy Dick's final gift to the library: for years he had spent St. Patrick's Day at this historic building, presenting recordings of his beloved music for all to enjoy, and adding in stories about McCormack—a man well known for his humor.

I recently went in search of this collection at Portland's three-story Central Library, now adjacent to a MAX train track covering thirty-three miles from Gresham in the east to Hillsboro of the west, and where some Portland homeless find a quiet, dry shelter during daytime hours. A library still with card catalogues and quiet rooms with shelves bursting books. A library where I was amazed to discover as a teen, shelves and shelves of musical scores that could be checked out simply with a library card. And although on this date so many years after Daddy Dick's donation, I had found a single program identifying the gift, I learned that the library had sold its collection, the records. Vinyl records more valuable in sale to make room for the digital recordings of modern times.

IRISH MUSIC HAUNTS my memory and accelerates the beating of my heart. "Toora Loora Loora" is the melody of my daydreams, summoning memories of river times long ago: mingling with the gurgling and babbling of the river. Last year I found myself in a remarkable Dublin music store where a young salesman recommended that I purchase a four-volume Irish tenor collection. Listening to the music, I drifted back over miles and years and generations.

Newly returned from Ireland, I played the CD as I drove alone from Portland to Eastern Oregon's Pendleton, navigating Interstate

84 through the magnificent Columbia River Gorge, a canyon that stretches over eighty miles. A gorge created during the last ice age when the Missoula Floods cut the steep walls framing the tremendous Columbia River.

I was still raw from Dad's death just two months prior. As if I were only now hitting adulthood. Passing by iconic Multnomah Falls evoked a long-ago memory—a visit with my parents, me a teenager of the 1970s. A spontaneous Saturday winter morning drive to visit the falls: partially frozen at the edges of the river. Frost covered tree branches. Icicles adorned roof eaves, forming sparkly, dangerous points beginning to drip onto the decking. Dad and I each devoured a Danish, he and Mom sipped black coffee, and I nursed a cup of cocoa with a huge dollop of whipped cream. I finished off the cream and asked for a second helping. It was cozy. And though it was sandwiched in between what I remembered as so much bad, it was good. And, I had forgotten.

And, yes, as I drove I listened to the Four Tenors perform "The Old Man." I drove on, miles still to cover along the Columbia River: nonstop tears dripping, sleeves soggy from wiping my face. Dad had died. His passing created a jagged-edged hole in me, lying vacant. I felt so childlike—couldn't he just come back? What could we have done differently? How could he be gone? Dad who shared the stories—the holder of treasured family lore, who made the river come alive. Dad who, at fifty and just a few years after that special Danish and hot chocolate, so bravely faced his demons. Dad who wrote letters: letters of advice, admiration, apology, condolence, and congratulation. Precious letters. This titan of the Willamette River. A man bursting with old river days: days of steamboats and music and exploration. How could I move on?

IT HAD BEEN a late June evening earlier that year when I took Dad and Mom to see their favorite musical at a local theater. *The Music Man.* I wasn't sure when I first asked Dad if he would like to see it, planning ahead two months to buy tickets. In these later years he often passed on theater, happy to have me and Mom enjoy it without him, and to be left alone to listen to music on the stereo—satisfied, even, with the elevator music available on Comcast television. But this time he enthusiastically agreed to attend, reminding me that *The Music Man* was his all-time favorite.

"Seventy-six trombones led the big parade . . ." he sang, his right arm pumping in and out; hamming it up . . . to the end.

As we sat through the show that night, I didn't know it would be our last to enjoy together. We rarely ever do. This musical that Mom and Dad had shared together from far back in their days as young lovers; its record spinning on their turntable for decades after. When Marian and Professor Hill began their love song, "Till There Was You," a now-grown Emily nudged me. Mom and Dad had instinctively reached for each other's hands. Clasped hands, adding to the bucket of memories etched within my heart. My Music Man.

CHAPTER 6
THE FALLS

WE GREW UP with a framed print of Dr. John McLoughlin hanging above our parents' bed; the print now collects dust in my garage, awaiting a new wall on which to perch. I was convinced through my childhood that Dr. John was a close family relation, while Dickie thought the white-haired guy in the painting was God.

Mom, Dede, Dad, Andy, 1967

Daddy Dick published a book about McLoughlin in 1934. *The White-Headed Eagle* was the first of three books he published about history, including *Young Northwest*, which targeted young readers. In a writing schedule hard for me to imagine, Daddy Dick worked three weeks on, three weeks off, writing evenings and weekends around his day job and his other great love, broadcasting evening book chats on radio station KEX. He used the proceeds he earned through book sales to "buy up," moving farther up Northwest Thurman Street, closer to the depths of Forest Park.

Daddy Dick radio book chat, ca. 1935

Late in his life in 1974, Daddy Dick was interviewed about his life and work by the Oregon Historical Society along with his sister, Frances Anne Montgomery Brewster—or Aunt Nan. These two siblings had grown up in the house near the drinking fountain on Portland's Northwest Thurman Street. While my great-aunt Nan spoke about her childhood and the Oregonian society column she wrote during World War II, it is her words about William Willson and Chloe Clarke that she seemed to have most proudly shared. And although Daddy Dick spoke about his jobs—assistant general manager for the J.K. Gill Book Company, district director of the Office of Price Administration during the war, and finally leading his own advertising agency—his writing and our early family stories were what he most emphasized in his still-available Oregon Historical Society recording.

"Must of the stuff on McLoughlin was historically correct but terribly dry reading," Daddy Dick offered. "I wanted to tell a story that was historically accurate but that would still make the man a human being." One book reviewer had criticized his book as an overly enthusiastic view of Dr. John—although it was the first book published about him to become popularly read. Daddy Dick believed his book had never received feedback from the Oregon Historical Society when it had been published, four decades before this interview, because the Society favored its own publications.

"We all think we are important, I guess, but we are only relatively so," Daddy Dick concluded.

Two decades after Daddy Dick's interview and his death, my daughter, Erin, selected Dr. John McLoughlin as the Oregon historical figure she would embody for her fourth grade project at Cedaroak Park Primary, a West Linn elementary school north of the falls of Oregon City and a mere stone's throw from the Willamette River. In a now-dated VHS recording, Erin sports white cotton hair peeking out from under a black bowler hat, a too-large white button-down shirt, and wire-frame spectacles. She addresses questions about "his" life, queried by her six-year-old sister, Emily, who proudly plays the part of a millennia-era news reporter wearing a white blouse and navy skirt, her trademark side ponytail popping up like a waterfall.

"Why are you so impotant?" asked the perky "reporter" who couldn't yet pronounce her r's.

"I treat Indians equally and I am peaceful. I give Indians the same punishment as white people. I have kept things peaceful. I also founded Fort Vancouver," recited "Doctor John."

The "reporter" tried to keep a straight face. "Tell me about yo wife?"

"Doctor John" gave the "reporter" a quick frown. "I predict my wife Marguerite will die several years after me. She opens her house to the needy and is thought of as one of the kindest women in the world."

"What do the Indians think about you?" asked the "reporter," concentrating hard, scribbling nonsensical looping doodles onto her notebook.

"The Indians love me for my kindness, justice, and fairness. But they sometimes fear me. They gave me the name the White-Headed Eagle."

"How do you feel?"

"I am convinced that I prevented a British-American war. I have compassion for everyone. I find it a terrible change to be a private citizen and to be sometimes disliked. I am very lonely and bitter, and my friends are worried about my despondency state," "Doctor John" said, capping *despondency state* in a ten-year-old's finger quotes.

And then, the final, unusual last question, asked by the animated "reporter." "How do you think you will feel when you die?"

"I think that when I die at age seventy-three in 1857, I will be a sad man. My nephew will ask me how I am going, and I will answer in French, 'Adieu.' To God."

The young "reporter" smiled, and the video cut to a movie that had been taped over.

THOUGH DR. JOHN was not family to us when my great-great-great-grandfather, William Willson, arrived in 1837—leaving New England to travel around Cape Horn on the ship *Diana*—he kindly received William Willson and his fellow missionaries at Fort Vancouver. William was born in Charleston, New Hampshire, and joined this voyage at age thirty-one. He left a life as a mariner and whaler back East and joined the mission as one of the first lay workers. I am not certain what it was that appealed to William for him to choose missionary living. Although he did carry the missionary agenda close to his heart, having been a member of Reverend David Leslie's church in Fairhaven, Massachusetts, perhaps his imaginings of an unspoiled West and the challenge of adventure further propelled him into this journey. He traveled alongside Dr. Elijah White, and Anna Maria Pittman—who went on to marry Reverend Jason Lee—among other travelers.

William Willson

Since William worked onboard alongside Dr. White and read the doctor's medical books onboard, this very informal but not then-uncommon education prepared him for later medical practice. William, in later years, was sometimes referred to as "Dr. Willson"; he'd learned enough medicine to provide some level of medical attention to those in early Oregon. Although one reference today describes him as an "eccentric cat lover" and a "medical quack," others wrote of Dr. Willson as a "highly likable man with terrific stories," especially those of the sea.

Up the wild Columbia the travelers on the *Diana* sailed, from its mouth at the Pacific Ocean. After enjoying hospitality provided by Dr. John at Fort Vancouver, the missionary party traveled by one boat and three canoes to take the passengers and their baggage up the Willamette River, the paddling done by William, Mr. Whitcomb, Mr. Lee, and a few Native Americans. At night they camped upon the river bank within groves of oak trees, eating salmon and potatoes. Finally, they arrived at the powerful Willamette Falls, where the local Indians determined the price of portage around the falls to be five charges of ammunition and a large cotton handkerchief for the chief. They continued on their way upriver until they reached the landing of Baptiste Desportes McKay at Champoeg, about fifteen miles from the Oregon Mission, the first and best known of the early Methodist missions. Soon after, William and two other men set back by canoe for several trips to transport the goods from the *Diana*.

William had been assigned as mission carpenter and kept busy building accommodations for the slowly growing settlement, and supporting other needs: sadly, he performed one of the last services for Anna Maria by building her casket when she died following childbirth in 1838. As Jason Lee continued to plan for the expansion of missions into the West, William and Reverend David Leslie traveled north to begin building a mission house in Nisqually, located then within the Oregon Territory, today's Puget Sound in Washington State. William continued to support the Methodist missions as a carpenter while he awaited the arrival of the missionary reinforcement.

Just three years after William arrived in Vancouver, my great-great-great-grandmother, Chloe Clarke, owner of the melodeon, arrived with fifty-one other Methodist missionaries aboard the *Lausanne* as part of the Great Reinforcement. They had traveled 22,000 miles across water in this new four-hundred ton, first-class sailing ship complete with spacious staterooms and that carried—in addition to passenger belongings—a sawmill, gristmill, and other farm tools and building materials. Food and household supplies added to the total expedition cost of $42,000.

As the *Lausanne* lay in anchor just east of the mouth of the Columbia, Dr. John, referred to as the Chief Factor, sent them fresh bread, butter, milk, and vegetables—all a welcome change after their nine-month sea diet. The reinforcement took ten days to slowly move ninety miles up the Columbia to Fort Vancouver, headquarters of the Hudson Bay Company, as they navigated unknown channels and were restricted by winds.

For us descendants, it seems lucky that Jason Lee settled his troupe of missionaries in the Willamette Valley, rather than among the Flathead Indians as he'd originally planned—lucky that William and Chloe, upon arriving separately, both received assignments in Nisqually.

A tough eight-day journey carried Chloe as she joined Dr. John Richmond and his family over the 150 miles from Fort Vancouver to Fort Nisqually. The Nisqually Branch Mission served as the earliest of local Protestant efforts and the northernmost of the five Jason Lee Methodist Missionary Stations, which also included Willamette Falls, Clatsop, The Dalles, and the most favored and largest, Willamette. Nisqually Mission was located in what is today Dupont, Washington, with its school, Chloe Clarke Elementary. To get there, Chloe's small missionary group canoed fifty miles down the Columbia and spent two days navigating up the Cowlitz River. As the missionaries camped along the Cowlitz, American Indians whooped and sang, surrounding them and introducing them to the West. After departing from the river, the missionaries traveled three more days overland in carts and horses, and finally were welcomed by a Hudson Bay Company representative at Fort Nisqually.

Dr. Richmond was responsible for conducting regular worship while Chloe prepared to fulfill her duties as mission teacher. Soon after arriving, Chloe met William, who was finishing building the mission. William and Chloe lived in the fort for three weeks while he completed its rather simple construction. Chloe prepared to teach whatever Indian children she could reach, sometimes as many as fifty—although the Indian population had already begun to dwindle due to the introduction of new diseases by white visitors. During the eighty-year period between 1770 to 1850, smallpox, measles, influenza, and other diseases had killed an estimated 28,000 Native Americans in Western Washington, leaving fewer than 10,000 survivors.

My great-great-great-grandparents married just thirty-seven days after Chloe's arrival in Nisqually. Although some may speculate that the two may have known each other from their previous lives in the Eastern United States, this isn't supported by family lore. And Chloe didn't appear to keep or save a journal from her earliest days at Nisqually. One year later she mentions the anniversary of this event, with reference to her "sweet husband."

"Sweet and sacred has been the peace and happiness which I have enjoyed in the society of one of the best of husbands . . . may we labor together successfully in the yoke of Christ."

I choose to naively believe this was some type of "love at first sight"—although I imagine the marriage was equally hurried by isolation, loneliness, and for Chloe, a sudden realization of what the 1840s West offered her, a single white woman. Their union was the first marriage within Puget Sound of a white man to a white woman, referred to as the "first American marriage," united by Dr. Richmond. Though Dr. Richmond would find life at Nisqually to be more than he had bargained for and soon return eastward with his family, Chloe and William made the West their home.

Nine months later, Chloe became very ill and gave birth to a premature baby. "God has permitted us to hold it in our embrace three short days and then in mercy relieved the little sufferer of all its pains and took it to himself." She thanked God for bringing her up from the gates of death. "The Lord has spared me a little longer, the brittle thread is still lengthened out," wrote my barely-twenty-three-year-old great-great-great-grandmother.

Just a month after the loss of her baby, in June of 1841, Chloe and William received orders to move to the Willamette Falls Mission, at the base of the glorious "Walamet Falls." It was a difficult journey south—William was thrown twice from his horse and they encountered trouble with Indians. When they finally arrived at the Falls, Chloe thanked God for bringing her safely through danger, as she was shaken up following the attacks by Native Americans on the mission at Nisqually.

Chloe wrote: "Dangers stand thick and all around to hurry mortals to the tomb. We will trust in the living God who alone can deliver in time of trouble."

Today, we are not fully sure where Chloe and William lived during their almost three years at the Falls, though William is listed in the 1842 census next to the listing for Reverend Alvin Waller in Oregon City. When they arrived, there may have been as many as four houses near the mission and the falls. This census, conducted by Dr. Elijah White of all those Americans living in the Oregon Territory in 1841 to 1842, listed people in "neighborhood order" with most people residing in French Prairie, Wailatpu—near today's Walla Walla—and Oregon City. William is listed along with one female over eighteen— our Chloe—along with seven horses, two neat stock, and ten hogs in our earliest Oregon City. Soon after, by December of 1842, the missionaries began building the first church in Oregon Country, at Willamette Falls, which was completed in 1844.

HOW DIFFERENT FROM today that June at Willamette Falls must have been. As cottonwoods, even then, sent out their pungent blasts of spring, absent was today's cacophony of noises—engines puffing along Oregon City rail tracks, and cars roaring along Interstate 205, Jet Skis in the river below. But oh, the Falls: soon to be the "End of the Oregon Trail."

I admire the Falls of today, not quite in their full glory, yet majestic still. I try to imagine how they looked in the mid-1800s.

"As they break over huge rocks in a spume of white spray and to see the fish, shining silver, jump up the waters is a sight that I wish I might share with my dear sister," wrote Chloe.

Chloe began making shirts for the local American Indians— although so many had been lost through disease, three hundred or so still gathered at the Falls during the season of salmon, from January through August. Native Americans within the lower Columbia and throughout the Willamette Valley had suffered greatly from the "Cold Sick"—an especially deadly influenza outbreak between 1829 and 1832. Although the Falls Tribes were not completely destroyed, the epidemics of this disease and others significantly impacted their numbers.

The missionaries found they needed to go to the lodges to share their beliefs with the Native Americans. The alternative was to pay the Indians to come to the mission—clearly Native Americans weren't begging to learn about Christianity. William was gone a good deal as he traveled to the coast to build the Clatsop Mission, near today's Astoria. Chloe wrote regrettably, in letters and in her diary, that she wasn't more useful or more holy. She was discouraged in her attempts to learn the Native American languages, as she realized how each tribe spoke their own, and she could never keep up given the different tribes then surrounding the Willamette Valley. She was also discouraged by the nomadic life of the people during the one week she might have them in school but knowing that the next week the same students might be twenty to thirty miles away.

Chloe's optimism seeped away as the missionaries' Christian messages failed to make an impact among the native people. "Our prospects for doing good in this land are very dark," she scribed. "Rum is being sold here and we fear very much harm will be done by ardent spirit, and the spirit of the Lord will not long inhabit the same body together." Chloe was afraid and looked to God to protect her from "the dart of the arrow, the stab of the knife." She wrote, "We know not when we lie down to sleep but we may be waked by the war whoop. Send down thy spirit" and let these tribes be "gathered into thy fold." Chloe prays, "O thou who hast promised to be with thy servants to the end, be with them, and give edge to thy truth, and let it find its way, even to the wildest savage's heart. O Lord bless our enemies and make them thy friends!"

I recoil as I read a descriptor she routinely chooses. My blood. My inheritance. Our past.

AS TIME PROGRESSED, new dangers emerged at the Falls. Many people drowned: Chloe wrote about a canoe carrying a few missionaries and Indians crashing over the falls. She particularly grieved with this loss, as three of those drowned had been boarding with her and they included two of Reverend David Leslie's daughters. Around this time, William broke a rib while handling timber on the river and his body began breaking down—old for his years. Relations with the locals weren't going well—one tribe threatened to destroy the mission, perhaps beginning to understand the loss ahead and the plans of white people.

Nearby, Dr. John watched the Methodists carefully, suspicious, as a Canadian, of the American missionaries' intentions as some began to rally for the United States' interests in Oregon. Some say Dr. John built his house in its original location partly to keep tabs on the Americans. Still, he was willing to help all newcomers, providing supplies without which many may have perished after the long journey over the Oregon Trail. Today, Dr. John's house remains, though it's been moved higher up, on a bluff in the heart of the town he founded: Oregon City.

Oregon City, where my brothers and I purchased chocolate-dipped cones from Dairy Queen on steep 7th Street after swim lessons. The home of nearby Wally's Music Shop, where we received the sweet reward of selecting a musical instrument to rent upon finally reaching the fourth grade. It's an old city with an old elevator to carry you from Main Street up to the bluffs looking over the Willamette River and, on a clear day, out to Mt. Hood in the east. The elevator runs even today, still with an operator, even though the view is quite different.

In 1840, before even the earliest of the Oregon Trail trekkers arrived, only a few hundred whites lived in the whole Oregon Territory. A letter sent by Dr. Jason Lee to the House Committee on Foreign Affairs in 1839 reveals a population census most of us who now call this place home could scarcely imagine: 151 American—or white—bodies, including about forty-five men settling as farmers, many married to Indian women and some with children fully grown. This letter was an early request from the Oregon Territory to our U.S. government to support settlers who were trying to expand into the West. Meanwhile, England—and Dr. John—hoped to savor the Territory as a place where elk and beaver would continue to reign: to be hunted by the English. The Donation Land Claim Act was established not long after, although it seems so alien now. It allowed a settler to claim hundreds of acres of fertile land by agreeing to settle for four years. *Come, people, come. But only whites need apply.* As the battle for land heated up, many still believed England would be able to acquire the land north of the Columbia River.

Early pioneers of the Oregon Territory petitioned the United States to offer aid and protection in this then-isolated wilderness, but as still common today, Congress delayed making any decisions. Finally, the settlers, including our William, were compelled to form their own independent government. Oregon: never dominated by another country or purchased or acquired, but colonized by settlers sitting under an American flag. A pronouncement often shared proudly in Oregon history, but not always with an acknowledgment of the original Oregonians from whom we took it. Some early settlers moved on, some preferred to roam, while others stayed and began to build what we know today.

AROUND THE TIME of Chloe and William's first years in the Oregon Territory, people paid for what they needed by exchanging beaver skins and wheat, and sometimes creating other tokens to symbolize parts of dollars. That is, until gold dust was introduced in 1848. Gold! People began carrying pouches of gold dust; a pinch equaled a dollar. Of course, a pinch is relative, so stores began introducing scales. But still, to many, gold dust didn't seem like a satisfactory system. So just prior to the new governor Joseph Lane taking office in Oregon, the Provisional Legislature of Oregon authorized the building of a mint in Oregon City in 1849. And William was elected melter and coiner.

However, politics of the past are not unlike those of today, and before long the new territorial governor claimed the proceeding illegal and the coins unconstitutional. In response, William joined others—including Oregon's first provisional governor, George Abernethy—to form the Oregon Exchange Company in Oregon City and start a mint. They melted gold dust, removed the impurities, and minted five- and ten-dollar coins with the stamp of a beaver instead of an eagle. Beaver money. In all, about $58,000 was coined, each coin carrying the mark of the beaver and the last name initial of each of the mint's owners. Eventually, the U.S. government worked to buy the coins up at a premium rate in exchange for U.S. currency, with most of the coins called up by the San Francisco Mint and taken out of circulation.

THE SEARCH FOR power generation in the West had begun in 1832, when Dr. John blasted a channel into the rock to carry the swift water to drive the millrace near Oregon City to power the first sawmill. In 1873, two decades after Chloe first sat at the edge of the Falls and a century before my own childhood, the Willamette Falls Canal and Navigation Locks opened with its Leonardo da Vinci design. Construction of the locks—our country's first multi-lift navigation locks—provided a much-needed navigation route around the mighty Falls. Steamboats and leisure boats alike could now safely pass between downriver and upriver locations. These locks were added to the National Register of Historic Places in 1974. And a decade after the opening of the Locks, in 1889, the energy of the Falls was harnessed as electricity, and pumped across fourteen miles to light lamps in downtown Portland.

Andy, Dede, Pat, Dad

TODAY I LOOK into the grandeur of the Falls across the river from my hometown of West Linn. I close my eyes and remember . . .

I was a little girl. Dad was in his white, billed captain's hat steering our boat, my brothers and I mesmerized by the spray of the river and the wake we generated as we headed downriver on a special Saturday. We left the flatter, less rippled downriver section of the Willamette, passing the Canby Ferry where it floated a crossing between Canby and rural Stafford. Shortly after we passed the mouth of the Tualatin, a river rippling with a few rapids before spilling into this section of the Willamette and inviting us to stop off at West Linn's Willamette neighborhood. But, instead, onward we motored toward the Falls near the southern bank of the river, just outside Oregon City. Dad pulled the boat far left, steering us into the narrow locks on the West Linn side.

Dad grabbed the ropes as we moved down, level by level, toward the water below: first, into the holding tank—the gate dropped and water spilled out, lowering our boat almost twenty feet. Dad grabbed a new rope, and we did it again.

"I'm not here to work," he said, a smile curling his lips. Four times we repeated the gate drop. Water spilled and we lowered the boat. Finally, we could freely move downriver.

We cruised, relaxed, passing between the still-quiet towns of West Linn and Oregon City, heading north past Milwaukie and Lake Oswego, until it was time to turn around, to repeat the locks process: this time moving upriver to join the water above the Falls and return home.

TODAY, I WALK alone midway across the arched, historic Oregon City Bridge. A bridge spanning the Willamette River between my hometown of West Linn and our neighboring Oregon City. Oregon City, a place that once dwarfed Portland in importance. I stand stock still on the south side of the bridge, staring down into the water, straining to imagine salmon. To my right is the still-operating West Linn Paper Company, its docks lining the river, and adjacent, the closed locks. To my left, the recently shuttered Blue Heron Paper Mill: soon to be revitalized in efforts to memorialize the industrial, cultural, and natural history of this historically rich space complete with a river walk. A mill with roots back to 1842 that we believe included our William's name on its original title.

Farther ahead on my left is the white water of the crashing Falls. The same Falls that Dad, during the last two years of his life, gazed at from the road below his new apartment in West Linn. I close my eyes—and re-open them. I imagine the rebuilding of legacy and heritage. Of something done right. To honor what once was.

CHAPTER 7
DANGEROUS LIVING

DAD'S FATHER'S SIDE of the family—through Daddy Dick–passed to us our earliest Oregon roots through Chloe and William. But it was Dad's mother's father, Ard Haradon, who introduced Dad to his earliest explorations of the Willamette River. This is all a bit ironic, as Ard, or "Pop-Ard" to Dad, was not a favorite to most in our family.

Ard was a rough character who never met Portland's high society standards. When Dad was young, Ard owned a gentleman's farm near Butteville, a town on the south bank of the Willamette River not far from today's Champoeg State Heritage Area. Butteville was established by Methodists during William and Chloe's era and competed for steamboat traffic and trade with the town of Champoeg in the late 1800s, but now sits as a mostly ghost town. Today the Historic Butteville Store tempts locals and visitors traveling to nearby Champoeg Park with local brew, ice cream, and snacks. But in Dad's childhood of the late 1930s, Pop-Ard's Butteville farm introduced Dad to a horse named Nick and freedom to explore.

At ten, on acres and acres of Wilsonville farmland along this southern Willamette River bank, Dad rode this trusty horse, whose full, given name—Nicodemus O'Malley—was that of a 1930s comic character. Our dad would hoist his small body up on Nick only after scrambling up on an old stump to be able to reach the horse's back. And Dad and Nick rode, exploring the open fields and pastures of this rural haven.

Later in the day after working up a thirst, Dad left Nick to track down his waterlogged rowboat that was docked on the river below the farm. He must have looked a bit like a comic character himself as he rowed with his dog—no life preserver back then—across and down the river to Red's Tavern to buy some soda pop. Dad wasn't able to row back upriver, instead hitching a ride back up to the farm on log rafts belonging to the local paper companies. That rowboat was Dad's first boat of oh so many.

On these weekend visits, Dad would eat breakfast with his Pop-Ard before his grandfather left for work, first as a sheet metal laborer during the war and later as a Northwest Portland candy factory owner. Pop-Ard was a joker and storyteller with an occasional lesson for Dad. "Don't forget, Dickie. A truly accomplished man can do two things: bake bread and build a fence." Dad followed half of that advice; fences he built.

In addition to introducing Dad to the Willamette, Pop-Ard fostered Dad's love of railroads, which later inspired him to create two of his own model railroads. The first was when I was a wee baby in my first Portland house, before we needed the railroad space for our growing family in our Wilsonville home.

The last was when we were all grown and Dad was finally retired. True to his love of storytelling, he wrote long, detailed tales about the fictitious town he brought to life to accompany his railroads. Our dad's late-in-life model Montgomery Family Railroad tracks encircled the town of Zenith, complete with a port, shipyard, and longshore workers, a fire tower and a lighthouse perched high above, and a village with grand hotel, shops—even a red-light district. He designed tiny shops named for kids and grandkids, with stores and services specifically selected to match our interests. He told me he liked thinking I was the one perched up in the fire tower, almost hidden in the mountain of fir trees high above the track. Down at the shipyard, longshore workers picketed for better wages as Zenith's Mayor dropped by in an attempt to calm workers during labor disputes. A YouTube video still exists of this railroad, holding the magic of Dad's trains perhaps for time immemorial, or perhaps until digital movies give way to the next technology.

Pop-Ard whetted Dad's appetite for trains after reclaiming two old Portland streetcars and moving them to this hillside farm property. Dad got the not so riveting task of helping to clean them out, abetting his grandfather's dream of an exciting new adventure. And although when I was little, I had imagined inhabiting a boxcar just like the characters in *The Boxcar Children* book series, living in a couple of old streetcars for Pop-Ard and my great-grandmother, Delia Holmes Harradon, or Muna, didn't turn out to be very romantic. It was cold and uncomfortable, and before too long, they moved back to Portland.

Frank, Dorothy, Delia, and Ardelia Haradon,
Seaside, Oregon, 1912

But the deal was already sealed: Dad was in love with the river. In this way, Pop-Ard introduced Dad to this greatest joy, our winding Willamette. But Pop-Ard also introduced Dad to his greatest life challenge. Before and after the move back to Portland, Pop-Ard would sit with Dad, sharing sips of Old Crow as he vivaciously told stories.

In 1930, the year my own father was born, Pop-Ard entered a guilty plea in federal court. He served two years in the McNeil Island Federal Penitentiary near Steilacoom, Washington—a site made famous by the Birdman of Alcatraz a few decades earlier. Ard was charged with using the mail system to defraud: eight others similarly charged were exonerated. This group of men sold false mortgages to banks and obtained false financial statements to make the mortgages appear valid. The details were widely shared in print in the Portland *Oregonian*, deeply embarrassing my grandmother WhoWho, then a young woman whose earliest beginnings were on a farm outside Helena, Montana.

In spite of, or perhaps because of this memory, WhoWho adopted a favorite phrase at least to us grandkids to "live life dangerously." She never told me about Pop-Ard and his prison time. Perhaps it was too painful for her, or perhaps, by that time, it just didn't matter anymore. Nor did she ever share with me the tragic fatal fall of her younger brother, under her watch, at Tillamook Head. Of that, I am certain, she never forgave herself.

Ard moved on to be the charismatic, storytelling grandfather Dad knew and loved, but he never returned to his pre-prison cocky self. Dad's other grandfather, William Montgomery, still referred to Ard as "a most despicable man." Pop-Ard remained Dad's confidant and filled Dad's brain with early Portland river adventures, even after suffering a stroke. For me, Pop-Ard's adventurous spirit lived through his daughter, WhoWho. And although others were challenged in their relationships with both Ard and his daughter WhoWho—she who did find a way through life by controlling others—it is ultimately the special relationship I had with my grandmother that endures in my memory.

WHEN I WAS little, I cried myself to sleep. I didn't want to die someday. Some promised something better after death—but life was good to me. I loved it. One night I calmed myself as my small child brain reasoned that, so far, the people I knew who had died were old.

"By the time I am old, someone will discover a cure for death," I whispered to myself each night as I tossed in my sheets and awaited sleep's comfort.

Now, in middle age, my adult brain understands that not only is there no cure, but that most of us wouldn't want eternal life in our bodies. Yet still. None of us knows what happens to those we love after they die. Whether we simply continue to feel them through our memories of the stories and love they shared while they were living; whether their essence hovers near us. Shortly before WhoWho died when I was in my early twenties, I kissed her, and though she was in a stroke-induced coma, her lips moved to kiss me in return. I want to believe she sits as an angel in front of me. I want to believe Dad hovers nearby, complementing her. These days, as I make my way along the shore of the Willamette—opposite the majestic Falls, through West

Linn's Mary Young State Park, along Portland's Esplanade—I do hear echoes of Dad. "What a river!"

IN THE 1960S, exploring without an adult tagging along was part of most kids' lives. For us siblings, poor choices—or sometimes just rotten luck—initiated frequent trips to Portland's Good Samaritan Emergency Room, rarely accompanied by much worry or haste. It may have been a fall off the rope swing as it arched over the river that left Andy with the first of a number of activity-induced concussions as he struck a tree on the bank. Or the time Dickie got his leg stuck riding double on a bike, returning home from the emergency room with a cast almost to his hip and introducing us to the seemingly disgusting therapeutic wonder of suppositories. Nothing seemed too worrisome to our parents as long as we stayed out of the river. Although they were lenient on many things, we kids learned early absolutes about swimming in a river when adults weren't around. At least until we were old enough to prove our strokes.

When Dickie was two, he fell off a gangway and plopped into the Willamette River. He was trapped between our dock and a piling for a long minute, terrifying our parents. My little brother's story, however, is not as dramatic as that of Sam Gill—the baby brother of our great-great-grandfather, J.K. Gill—who also plopped off a deck and through a hatchway. For Sam, it was the deck of a ship in 1854, several days off the banks of Newfoundland. This one-year-old had just left England with his four older brothers and parents to come to America on the *William Tapscott*, part of the Black Ball ship line. At thirteen, Sam's eldest brother, J.K., was far more interested in watching all things nautical than keeping tabs on a baby brother crawling across the deck of the ship. Two decks below, an Irish woman was doing her washing when into her tub, full of clothes, water, and soap, plopped baby Sam.

"There's a baby in my bucket!" the woman hollered.

Baby Sam was pulled out of the water, no worse for the wear, and the family journey continued across the Atlantic to America.

"Fortunately, he received no harm, but he showed his dislike for soapy water by lusty screams which soon attracted my mother," wrote J.K. years later. Is it merely coincidence that this same Sam Gill, decades after creating such excitement aboard the *William Tapscott*, created a life engineering steamboats up and down Oregon rivers?

Some twenty years after the "baby in the bucket" as J.K. strolled along New York's East River, he spied the *William Tapscott* docked—the very same ship that had carried him and his family across the ocean. She was now a cattle ship with her passenger ship days behind her.

"Ahoy there!" J.K. called to a nearby deckhand. "Any chance we can come aboard for old time's sake?"

After hearing J.K.'s story, the deckhand agreed to ask the ship captain. As it turned out, the same Captain Bell still captained this ship, and upon remembering the bucket story, he invited J.K. and his brother aboard.

AS MY FAMILY prepared for our first summer living on the Willamette River in 1964, Mom enrolled in a senior lifesaving course. Her classmates were all teenage boys—Mom's pregnant silhouette made her an obvious outlier. Indifferent to her pregnancy status, Mom successfully earned her Red Cross Senior Life Saving Certificate, and we were all allowed a bit more freedom to enjoy our life on the river.

Though we all were subjected to swimming lessons, Dickie, the youngest, got the shortest straw.

"Why do I have to go here?" he asked, clinging to Mom's hand, reluctantly following her down the stairs toward the bowels of the original West Linn High School building, dark, quiet, with windowless cement walls. When they got to the pool, it presented itself as a frightening, scummy recipe, right up to the mold-infested tile steps.

"Come get in the water!" the unsmiling instructor ordered in a grim, faded, one-piece suit: a perfect creature to inspire drowning nightmares in tots.

"Why do I have to?" my little brother repeated, reluctantly dropping Mom's hand and slowly moving into the pool. He took the lesson, but perhaps it's no surprise that he hated swimming.

Even with swimming lessons, life jackets were the required uniform when we were in the water or on our boat until we were strong enough to swim against the current of the Willamette. We were eager to graduate from the orange canvas PFD's to the belted white ski preservers, though we didn't have any agreed-upon criteria we had to demonstrate for this graduation. Perhaps just enough begging to drive Mom crazy.

MANY DECADES LATER with the new millennium approaching, our now-retired Dad was invited to star in a local public service announcement as an advocate for river safety and personal flotation devices. The PSA was sponsored by big river players: Tidewater Barge Lines, Foss Maritime Company, Shaver Transportation Company, and Bernert Barge Lines. All involved were concerned about safety on the Willamette and Columbia Rivers with the increasing myriad of skiers, sailboards, personal watercraft operators, and rowers moving through the system alongside commercial boats. In this ad, Dad acted the role of a grandfather motoring a speedboat on the Willamette while being urgently advised to slow down by his cute, blonde "granddaughter," played by the star of multiple TV spots filmed that day.

"Thanks, kid. I always knew you were the smartest one in the family," Dad would recite, as directed.

To this, after every take for six hours, the fake granddaughter would scream, "You are not in my family!"

Later, after the filming was finally over, we watched the ad reel together. A very young Erin was irate. "Why is Pops playing grandpa to her? He is *my* grandfather! It should be me on TV with him."

Dad couldn't win. This eldest granddaughter still thought of herself as the only grandchild. Her Pops: the one who personally selected the first teddy bear to grace her bassinet. This granddaughter who learned to say "Pops" with a wide grin and an impish twinkle in her eye as together they shared their earliest nonverbal private jokes. In this short period of time, Erin had learned—as would the other grandkids coming up behind her—that it was Pops who was king of the river. And he was her grandfather.

CHAPTER 8
OUR TOWN

DOWNRIVER FROM CHAMPOEG but less than ten miles upriver from Willamette Falls lies my childhood town of Wilsonville: settled in 1846 by Alphonso Boone, grandson of Daniel Boone. My brothers and I grew up watching *Daniel Boone*, a late 1960s television series starring Fess Parker. And as they did with other jingles, my brothers changed the lyrics, creating crude versions of that theme song that I will never repeat.

At the time we didn't pay attention to the fact that Boone's family was part of the Great Migration across the Oregon Trail. Among my friends with early Oregon roots, our ancestors' arrival by ship was rare compared to the trek across the Trail. One friend—descendant of an Oregon Trail family—used to say the people with money were the ones who came by ship. Perhaps, even more than money, transportation back then was determined by who you knew. And, especially, by what you believed. For the early missionaries were among those who came by ship, beating the Great Migration on the Trail by several years.

In 1847, before he left for the California Gold Rush, Alphonso Boone started a ferry service across the Willamette River. For many years, his son, Jesse, operated the ferry: the roots of today's Boones Ferry Road, a busy thoroughfare connecting Wilsonville to the neighboring towns of Tualatin, Lake Oswego, and to Southwest Portland. Jesse operated that ferry until 1872 when he was gunned down at the south landing in a dispute with a neighboring settler—like a *Boone* episode straight out of our television set.

AS COLLEGE-BOUND students in the early 1950s, Mom and Dad traveled from Portland to their separate colleges: Mom to then-Oregon State College in Corvallis, and Dad to Eugene's University of Oregon, a town near the mountains of the Willamette River headwaters. When they traveled together back to college after visiting

Portland, they preferred the westside route, traveling across the Boones Ferry. Mom and Dad always loved ferry rides.

The modern Boone Bridge, just south of the landing on the Willamette, wasn't completed until 1954. If you get off that bridge today, traveling south from Portland to our capitol of Salem, you can still put your boat and toes in the water at Boones Landing on the south bank of the river.

JUST UP BOONES Ferry Road from the north side of Boones Landing sat our Wilsonville Elementary School of the late 1960s and early 1970s. Once or twice during my school days, on a particularly hot last day of school we visited that landing for a celebratory plunge.

"It's field day!" I would say over breakfast on the last day of school. It was my favorite day of the school year. I was so excited! Visions of three-legged races, wheelbarrow races, and gunnysack-jumping contests spun through my head. And ribbons. I coveted the blue ribbons. My friend Lynnette and I vied for the blue ribbons awarded to the top girl finishers. And those few times after: we waded into the river, still in our field day attire—the only day we were allowed to wear shorts and T-shirts to school.

It wasn't until years later, as an adult trading notes with an old classmate, that I regarded that day from a different perspective. At that point, our Wilsonville Elementary was being demolished, the site now ripe for even more shopping, frozen yogurt, and wireless stores in an ever-expanding Wilsonville, a town today with more than 23,000 people, three elementary schools, and both a middle and high school. Some of us, now adult graduates of that school—an eight-grade school that was the only school in all of Wilsonville during our childhood—were in the schoolyard celebrating memories one last time before the bulldozers hit. This was the first time some of us had seen each other since the long-ago decades of our childhood.

"Remember field day?" I asked as we stood on the playground. My daughters played alongside the kids of my now-grown classmates on swings and a slide: a colorful playground that met safety standards not yet crafted when I was a kid, back in the days of gray-only, wildly spinning, metal merry-go-rounds and high monkey bars.

"Oh yeah. I hated that day," my classmate Lisa said.

I looked at her. Surprised. "Really?" I couldn't believe someone hated my favorite day.

"Yeah, great for some of you—who won all the races," she said. "The rest of us dreaded it. Why would we have liked that?"

I had never thought of field day like that before—in term of merits determined by physical competition. I looked past the play equipment to the rail line just outside school property. I remembered putting pennies down on the track and coming out later to find them off in the bushes—flattened by the passing freight train. I looked for my old friend Keith's house across those tracks and instead saw rows of storage units. Farther past the playground, the baseball diamond still looked used. The same spot where I was first invited to be a base runner during Little League practice. I was distracted as I wondered what they would do with the baseball diamond when they bulldozed the old school.

I looked back at Lisa and reminded her about the last act on a few of those last days of school. And we did agree on one thing: on those particularly hot last days of school, we loved to go down to the river afterward. Plunging, jumping, splashing: in the river, a celebration for all.

I REFLECT BACK on our early days—this undeveloped, fertile land bisected by the emerald river; holly and filbert orchards mostly of yesteryear. From the very beginning, Wilsonville sat at a transportation crossroad. The Boones Ferry was one of the first Willamette crossings, linking trade and commerce between Portland and the Willamette Valley. In my childhood days, Wilsonville was a sleepy cow town, sparsely populated by hardworking farmers trying to make a living, and a few families like ours whose parents, mostly dads, made a living in Salem or Portland. But in its early days back in my great-great-grandparents' time, Wilsonville was a bustling port boasting steamers docked with passengers, wares, and crops transported up and down the river between Portland and southern lands, as far as Corvallis. Back then, even more dairies, hop yards, grain fields, and family farms dotted the countryside.

When the railroad built a new trestle in Wilsonville in 1907, businesses moved away from the riverbank to be closer to active rail connections. Trains made sixteen stops daily in Wilsonville, often hauling country kids to high schools in Portland. In 1968, Wilsonville—with a population of around a thousand people— became incorporated. The interstate freeway was completed while we lived in Wilsonville, allowing Dad and others like him to more easily commute to work. And my own older brothers only had a ten-mile bus ride to high school in West Linn. Although things were changing, Wilsonville didn't boast its own high school for another three decades after we moved away. A high school built in the woods of my childhood.

The sleepy Wilsonville I knew awakens during my nighttime dreams. And to me, as it was with Dad, the stretch of the Willamette upriver from Boones Landing is about the most special you can find on this grand river.

THE WILLAMETTE VALLEY is 150 miles long; at its heart, the Willamette River flows. The valley's fertility results from alluvial soils deposited across its broad, flat plain in the great Missoula Floods. Our valley was publicized in the 1820s as the "promised land of flowing milk and honey." The fertile lands of the Willamette Valley drew settlers with the promise of free land for white Americans willing to settle. Settle without the civilized cities of Missouri and New Hampshire. Our fertile soil: Oregon berries and timber. Today, vineyards add to the mix. Strangely, even living in this land of bread and honey, none of our generations of Oregon ancestors were real farmers. Drugstore and bookstore owners, teachers and writers, but no farmers beyond the gentleman garden and orchard.

My family inherited the remnants of an early orchard on our Wilsonville land: mature Bing and Queen Anne cherry trees; apples; a huge branching maple. The Bings—dark red and sweet—were my favorite cherries; created just downriver in Milwaukie back in my great-great-grandparents' day. A cherry named for the Chinese orchard foreman who wasn't again allowed into the U.S. after the 1882 Chinese Exclusion Act. We hauled ladders and climbed the branches of the cherry trees, preferring the fruit ripe from the tree rather than canned later in the winter. And our mom thrived in country living, having grown up during the Depression with an avid farming father who used their two lots in Northeast Portland to grow as much as they could to feed his large family of six daughters.

My Portland grandmother, a proud supporter of the Temperance Movement, wasn't quite as adventurous, though, and when visiting was sometimes fearful of what wild children we all were.

"Patty, what in the world are those children doing out there?" she would ask Mom.

Outside the kitchen window towered the grand maple tree, blasting us with red and orange and gold each fall. From the time we were preschoolers, Mike or I would climb up ladder steps on the huge trunk, while the other climbed a nearby self-standing ladder to synchronize the timing of two different rope swings: high up approaching the river bank, crisscrossing in delicate patterns, effectively timed to avoid smashing our heads together.

Mike on the maple

"They are fine," Mom would respond. Barely looking up at what we were doing. Believing in the need to be kids.

"Tsk, tsk." Grandma Daum would frown, shaking her head, before heading back to her usual place at the piano.

The vegetable garden and fruit harvesting were pretty much Mom's turf. Dad had strangely, it seems to me now, set his sights on creating a small Japanese-style garden in our front yard, complete with mounds. I still get itchy when I think of our weeding responsibilities in that garden: each of us required to keep a bark-covered mound weeded.

Dad did love being outside, and he was always eager to take on the traditionally "manly" outside tasks, though Mom was our plumber and electrician. He was a strong guy, happy to spend weekend mornings with a chainsaw or lawn mower.

KIDS GROWING UP in the Willamette Valley worked on farms or spent summer days berry picking and hay baling. We were no different. Except that our earnings filled our pockets and didn't help pay for basic family expenses. And for us, berry picking only lasted a few, sweet but sweaty, weeks. Those few weeks of summer we got up early, just as the sun was rising.

"Hurry up! It's almost six o'clock," Mom would call as she came into our bedrooms, issuing a more commanding reminder in person than over the intercom system.

An impossibly bad joke, we would think, lying in our beds dreaming of our summer vacation. But we were lucky. Mom packed us each a lunch, freezing cartons of less-than-one-hundred-percent juice so they stayed cold through the hot day, and drove us to the berry-picking bus stop in our school parking lot. To join a swarm of kids—most we knew, some we liked. We suffered through long, hot days, eating dirty berries on the sly.

"Pick your row clean!" field supervisors would bark, pacing up and down the gravel field road. "No moving off your row until it is inspected and clean!"

And then, as if out of nowhere, sometime before lunch, a ripe, red berry would sail through the air. One never hit me—guess I was lucky enough to be neither liked nor disliked enough to be the target of the ever-threatening berry war. And if a supervisor caught wind of the tossed berry, we would all hear the oft-shouted-and-repeated threat. "If I see you throw a berry, you can kiss your little summer money-making venture goodbye!"

The threat didn't seem to stop berry fights, instigated mostly by the oldest boys, inventing relief from the drudgery of picking and unconcerned with consequences. Usually they were worldly enough to figure out how to avoid getting caught.

But, oh, the joy of finally filling a crate, teeming with ripened red strawberries, the sweet scent emanating across the fields. No other strawberries on this planet taste like Oregon berries. Especially today. A berry not designed for shipment, peaking within hours of picking. A crate filled, we finally had permission to leave our row and walk to the keeper of the strawberry cart, receiving the reward of a punch on the card. And at the end of day, we could turn in our cards for cash. I don't remember liking or looking forward to the weeks of berry picking. It was just something everyone did. Until times and landscapes changed.

I wasn't astute enough, then, to try to conceive of the lives of those picking crops for a living: to support a family. I hadn't yet connected berry picking with survival, even though, in the Head Start class Mom taught in nearby Tualatin, all the students were children of Hispanic migrant farmers. I was invited to join Mom's classroom on the rare day she had class and I didn't. I still remember Pedro and his sister Maria, several years younger than me. I crudely tried to read to them in Spanish, using my tiny vocabulary learned piecemeal in school. I thought they were cute and I loved little kids. Soon after, though, Mom needed to visit their parents, and I tagged along. I knew nothing about labor housing. Though I had friends who were poor, the concept of living in a building with other families at a field that was worked during the day, sometimes by children, was beyond what I knew. I couldn't understand it—didn't then know the questions to ask.

WHEN WE GOT home from picking strawberries, we gratefully jumped into the river to wash off the dust, counting down the days till the berries were past their prime. Others might move on to raspberries and blueberries, or learn how to string green beans as Mom did as a kid in East Portland. But not us. Until filbert season, that is.

I didn't know what a hazelnut was until I was in college. We knew filberts—our childhood Wilsonville teemed with them. For us, filbert-picking season lasted only a few weeks every fall, as our neighbor, Mr. Colby, added us to the mix of paid labor in his acres of filbert orchards lining the river. I'm sure he offered this as the neighborly thing to do, rather than seriously thinking we would offer any real help toward his harvesting efforts. We weren't nearly as efficient as others, who had to make ends meet with their earnings. Though I imagine one thing was the same for all of us: the aroma of Mr. Colby's orchard in the Willamette Valley fall. That powerful potpourri of decaying apples, maple leaves, and unripened nuts. The sweet earthy smell of the green filberts, not yet dropped from the trees, is forever imprinted in me.

Each of us kids were armed with a metal bucket and gunnysack; rakes to share. Once a gunnysack was filled—though it seemed each new, empty bag would take a childhood—we successfully added a tag, writing in our name with a blue, ballpoint pen. Then, finally, we would receive our seemingly meager payment for a bag almost as big as me. I don't know that I ever earned money to buy much of anything during filbert season. I don't even remember ever fully filling a sack, though I must have. What I do remember is that Mr. Colby had the tastiest Red Delicious apples I have ever eaten. Never since have I tasted an apple that good. Though Mrs. Colby watched us unhappily from the house—probably she'd discovered one of my brothers was stealing filberts from unattended sacks—Mr. Colby didn't seem to mind us taking breaks to climb his trees and eat our juicy fill. A few apple trees surrounded by filberts, on the banks of the Willamette.

CHAPTER 9
MONKEY WRENCHING

AS KIDS, DICKIE and Mike liked best to play a game their infinitely wiser, older sister created.

"Do you want to play 'Boys,' today?" one of us would ask. Each of us adopted the same imaginary male name, with Dickie always choosing Tom Walker, and Michael referring to himself as Robert. For whatever reason, I usually chose the name Patrick, though brother Patrick never knew that until now. And we would fabricate an adventure in the nearby woods, meadow, or on the riverbank. Decades later I found the humor in my brothers joining in a game of make-believe named for their gender, following the lead of a sister who so often wished to be one of them. And as children of the 1960s, we would disappear, our parents trusting that this was what kids did, and everything would be okay.

Our house, mid-1960s

On an early summer day after a previous late-night shower decorated ferns and willows with a glossy finish, Dickie and I undertook our grandest adventure, the one we still talk about. Just like Lewis and Clark, we planned to trace the mouth of our river—really a creek flowing through our woods. Woods that a short time later would awaken our spirits to unspeakable acts. This day, though young and inexperienced, we knew that all creeks led somewhere. To join other larger bodies of water moving on a journey.

We tromped from our house to our fort, a few stale graham crackers stuffed in our pockets. From our fort we headed off in a yet-undiscovered—at least by us—route to the southeast. We made our own trail when the game trails dead-ended, staying as close to the creek as possible without getting soaking wet. That was our deal—we were, after all, following the creek. As the banks steepened we created our own portage, climbing around the backside of a sloughing cliff.

"Dickie," I yelled. "Watch! Who am I?" I half fell, half jumped off the cliff. Easily stopping before I landed in the creek.

"Ha," he yelled. "Watch me. I'm Butch Cassidy," he added and copied my jump.

We descended to catch up with the still-moving creek. Hours we continued on our mission, or was it really the child time of sixty minutes? But finally, the denseness of the forest ended. We saw sky as we neared a bank. A riverbank. Our tumbling, winding creek spilled out. Finally, it cascaded down the bank to the river we thought we knew so well, spilling into the sparkling liquid highway. We didn't know how far downriver we were from our own riverside home, not recognizing any features on the banks, with no buildings or homes to identify.

My brain no longer holds any remembrance of the trek home. Engraved in my memory, though, front and center, is the valiant pleasure of our own Corps of Discovery success. It was true. Everything did lead to the Willamette! We were jubilant in our explorations. Just like our own Dad, at the same age, decades before, just a few miles upstream.

NOT LONG AFTER that, the big day came. It was a Saturday. A day when everything we kids knew to be important stood starkly before us, awaiting our defense. It's not like we meant to cause trouble—we were basically good kids. Our parents had taught us to be polite and to respect others. But that day we were caught off guard. We were mad. Five of us between five and twelve years old, and me the only girl, as usual. We headed out on what we believed to be a usual day, to do usual things. We loved our fort, sharing a communal loyalty like all gangs of kids have to some special spot, whether an abandoned urban lot or a country paradise. Three dead, rotting logs covered with moss, a testament to our dense Pacific Northwest forests. They sat in nature's perfection, layered across the slope on our hillside. The ideal spot to hang out, plan adventures, and talk. I had already envisioned the club I would form if any other girls ever moved into the neighborhood, where we would dig out the crude clay lying in waiting in the earth, and make bowls and figures just like in art class. Below us at the base of the hill lay our navigated creek—rushing with the spring Oregon rains; dawdling later in the summer. Arising out of this kids' paradise was our lookout tree. A tree with branches sheared by late-night winter wind storms. Its rough trunk curved in a wide arch out over the creek, its remaining branches perfectly spaced for reaching arms and legs. We would climb and look out onto our land. Our place to be in the world. Our woods. Or so we thought.

While we were young and naive, we knew that adults disagreed about what should happen to our town and its land in our Wilsonville of the late 1960s—similar to conversations in other Western towns. Fewer than one-thousand people lived in our not yet incorporated, rural town. My dad and his sometimes-argumentative brother, Bill, our next-door neighbor, disagreed. Dad favored incorporation, designing the brochure illustrating Wilsonville as a "Quality Community with Potential Unlimited." My uncle, never one to be told what to do, was adamantly and vocally opposed. This same uncle would pull out his Civil War cannon replica, load it full of something simulating ammunition, and fire from the bank above the river on July Fourth. He was opinionated, and if pushed could be impolite and disrespectful. This uncle—like so many before and after him—did not like to be told what to do with his land. He won a seat on the Wilsonville City Council on the platform that he didn't vote for incorporation, even though it passed. Mayor Balsinger and Uncle Bill wrangled through the newly incorporated town meetings. This mayor believed thoughtful development was critical to advancing this land. My uncle and others were angry that some had decided to allow the development of Charbonneau, a then undesignated, undeveloped area just across the river from us. Charbonneau was to be the first of its kind: a planned development with large boundaries, all within some of the most fertile farmland of the valley. And even today, Charbonneau sits adjacent to still-undeveloped farmland targeted in embroiled, contentious land development debates.

As we headed to the fort that day, we spotted an intruder in our midst.

"What is the bulldozer doing here?" asked our group's twelve-year-old elder. The foreign metallic yellow contraption stopped us in our tracks.

We scratched our heads—what on earth was it doing here? We looked at each other. In all the elapsed minutes between then and now, I don't know how long we considered our next actions. We could have sat down, thoughtfully imagining all the alternatives to deal with this new finding. Perhaps we could talk to our parents, learn the facts, or just go on with our day. But no. We felt viscerally attacked. In our home. In our Eden. In our young minds, there were no property owners here. This was the woods. The woods that had always been as long as we could remember, and should always be.

We acted on impulse. Our only thought was to do whatever we could to prevent this heavy piece of equipment from threatening our space. We attacked it.

"Do you see that ax?" I asked Mike, referring to a pickax leaning against a tree.

He nodded and gave me an encouraging smile. I picked it up. I looked at all of them for courage and swung it hard at the dozer tires. I was little and although I knew how to swing a baseball bat, I wasn't graced by a satisfying pop as the ax struck the tire. Looking back, maybe I give us too much credit in actually damaging much of anything.

"Mike, what are you doing?" I asked as he took a rock and smashed the dial on the dashboard.

"Just helping," he said.

I have no memories of the acts performed by others, though I know we were all busy. Did someone try to pour sand into the gas tank? Perhaps that's something we thought up later, not sophisticated enough at the time to imagine that level of monkey wrenching. I did think Mike to be the smartest of all of us as he grabbed the key, still in the ignition, and threw it far into the bushes. Pleased with himself. None of us drove yet, but we all knew you couldn't start a car, and probably not a bulldozer either, without a key.

We were oblivious to any worries about being seen by anyone. We had never seen anyone else in the woods. And then we went home. That was it. None of us told any of the adults in our lives. But someone found out. And somehow they figured it was us. The fact my brothers and I weren't really punished leads me to believe our parents had at least a little empathy for our wild emotions. Or perhaps, in the thick of their own conflict, they had more than enough on their own plates.

Sometime after that, my younger brothers and their buddies found another nearby piece of equipment to terrorize—this time a tractor near the holly orchard down the street. They found humor, as only seven- and eight-year-olds can, in taking the key out of the ignition every evening and tossing it into the bushes. One night the tractor owner lay in wait and chased them far down the road toward our house. Today Rick, no longer Dickie, claims the kids successfully evaded their stalker, diverting their chase by running down a path toward the woods. Though I question this final ending, I know that elapsed time can be the best friend to coloring memories. Especially memories from childhood.

SOON AFTER WILSONVILLE incorporated, Governor Tom McCall coined his famous and contentious quip. "Come visit us again and again. This is a state of excitement. But for heaven's sake, don't come here to live." He and other Oregon leaders identified a long-range vision for land development, putting Oregon on the map as a leader in land-use planning laws. Decades of contentious debates had begun. McCall fought long and hard, and to his deathbed for these land protections. Today, half a century later, Oregon's Willamette Valley land arguments escalate. She attracts newcomers, pushing to create space, yet growing more crowded and congested. She struggles to create affordable housing in prime areas where developers might rather create luxury condos, and many others would prefer to keep wild. We live in the midst of pressing land-development squabbles to bring our own Stafford Basin within Portland's urban growth boundary.

I pass through the Wilsonville of today. I feel mournful. Where holly and filbert orchards once bordered Wilsonville Road, now I pass a mini-mall, concrete holding together electronics stores and fast food restaurants and car washes. Growth accommodates people and places, this spot next to our major interstate. I drive down to Wilsonville Memorial Park—barely half a river mile from our old home of the 1960s. I park and walk down to the muddy banks of the river. It seems at first that nothing has changed. But no, as we all learn, you can't ever fully return to your childhood. Even if on the surface it seems the same, life transforms everything.

CHAPTER 10
BOATS, CARP, AND STEAMERS

ONE OF MY favorite photos of my brother Rick was taken shortly after his late July birth, onboard the *Willamette Chief*, our grandparents' cabin cruiser. Daddy Dick named this boat, so much fancier than our motorboats, after the original stern-wheeler. On lazy weekends we would board, with Daddy Dick in his white-billed captain's hat, to explore the river, slower than in our motorboat and with more elaborately prepared lunches. I always loved how the *Chief* had room for a table toward the stern where we could eat even when moving, or play Go Fish when the boat was anchored.

WhoWho and Willamette Chief, 1966

When Daddy Dick captained his smaller motorboat, he went fast—especially near marinas. He generated frantic waves from those he passed—spectators gesturing, trying to warn him to slow down. My grandfather, grinning proudly, would wave back and say, "Everyone is so friendly on the river." Though a kind English gentleman, he wasn't truly an expert boater, evidenced by his white-knuckled landings and the dent created when he hit a well-marked rock near New Era Bar. Instead of recognizing his error, he threatened to lodge a complaint with the maritime board for allowing rock in the channel. But in the *Willamette Chief*, Daddy Dick drove like a gentleman, sedately touring the river.

In my favorite photo of Rick, I am a smiling four-year-old with my baby brother, then, Dickie, in my arms. My Dickie. The little brother Mom had promised would, in fact, be a sister. Back when he was born—a few weeks before this photo was taken—my parents called from the hospital in Portland to tell us about our newest brother. WhoWho, our caregiver while Mom was away, proudly announced this news to us kids. I remember slowly hitting my forehead against the basement stairwell, thinking how Mom had crushed my hopes. But by the time Mom and Dickie came home from the hospital, I had forgotten, so happy was I to have a new baby in our house. And Dickie became my project: I eagerly made plans to be the one to teach him everything he needed to know in life. And I figured, too, I could get him to do the things my other brothers weren't much interested in: play dolls and school.

My own memories of this boat trip, though, detail the tear tracks on my cheeks, not yet fully dried by the time the camera clicked its shutter. Pat and Andy were having great fun, jumping from the boat deck into the river, over and over and over. Yet my parents decided, even with my orange canvas life jacket that I was too young to jump into the current of the Willamette sweeping past our anchored boat.

I was furious. "That's not fair!" I objected over and over. I'd already begun to identify a pattern: stark contrasts between what my brothers and I were allowed. I did, however, love my baby brother, as my parents well knew. I treasured every opportunity to hold this live baby, rather than my lifeless dolls, even the ones with appendages fully attached. Dad and an occasional babysitter had already abused my love affair with Dickie by promoting me to Lead Dirty Diaper Changer when Mom was away. And for this moment on the *Willamette Chief*, by the time the camera shutter closed, I smiled, forgetting for a moment the injustice I suffered.

EXPLORING THE SMALLER tributaries of the Willamette River made us feel like we were in the same league as the early Oregon explorers. We could be Captain Gray, the first white man to cross the Columbia Bar and crawl up the Columbia River, or David Thompson scribing early maps for the Northwest Fur Company. I hadn't once been allowed to join my older brothers as they canoed down the Molalla River with WhoWho, certainly another injustice. And I wasn't old enough—or the right gender—to join their bad boy escapades with our cousins: outings that included canoeing to a beach they called Tortilla Flats to play soccer, a sport not yet well understood in the United States, with a lighted roll of toilet paper soaked in gasoline.

I will never forget, though, our motorboat ascent of the Yamhill River. Even Dad and Mom were especially excited on this voyage, making us feel a bit like the Swiss Family Robinson. None of us knew for sure, not even Dad, how far up the lower stretch of the Yamhill we could get, as Dad knew a dam blocked through-travel at some point. Dad exuded true happiness, always, when in a boat. And even in these years on the Willamette, while he may have had a beer, drinking to excess was not something he did when he was out in the outdoors with us. Dad loved his weekends. For us in those early years, they were family time.

Dad, Dede, Mike, and Dickie on the Yamhill River, 1969

As we motored up the river—so narrow compared to the Willamette—Dad steered to avoid the shallower points of the riverbed. Shallow areas where we could see the smooth, rounded river rocks visible through the water's surface. Midway, we pulled up to the bank, careful not to hit rocks with the prop, and Mike and I scampered up the bank on a trail that seemed to lead nowhere. Nobody around; no evidence of people at all. I found a place to pee before running back to the sandwich awaiting me on the shore. And we did eventually hit the dam, but not before discovering this new, seemingly uncharted territory, making us feel exactly like the explorers of long ago.

Mom with kids on the Yamhill River, 1969

A RIVER-LOVING family like ours maintained a procession of boats: Daddy Dick's *Willamette Chief;* Uncle Bill's boats—the *Marauder,* a fifteen-foot ski boat sporting a shark's face below the bow, and the *Rum Runner,* a Boston Whaler; WhoWho's *Mudhen,* a small rowboat with an outboard motor; Dad's childhood boat, the original *Walrus,* later replaced by the *Walrus 2,* a tiny model ship, followed by the *Walrus 3,* a canoe, and, finally, the *Walrus 4*—a decommissioned twenty-seven-foot Coast Guard Bartender.

Then there were the *DeDe*s. One of the few advantages of being a girl in this boy-saturated family was having boats named after me—the *DeDe* followed by *DeDe 2* after the original *DeDe* bit the dust. I liked knowing that my brothers had to ride in a boat that proudly shouted my name, adorned in basic black lettering. But if you happen to ask Patrick today, he will tell you that, upon the blessing of my own dad, Pat and Andy used a razor blade to obliterate those black letters during the last days we lived on the river, teen boy boat captains embarrassed to pal around soliciting my name. Instead, they added cheap gold lettering that spelled out *River Runner*. Sadly, I didn't think about this until after Dad's passing. I can only imagine what great fun he would have had helping me understand what got him to so undercut my power. I prefer to remember the *DeDe*s as I knew them, and the glorious feeling of knowing I had something my brothers didn't.

NEARLY EVERY FARMER back in Oregon's early days had his own dock along the river to serve as a shipping point for crops: there were thirty-eight landings toward the end of the 1800s located just between Butteville and Canby—over the distance of a mere nine river miles. Boats brought all types of supplies to farmers' docks, leaving again with lumber, produce, and even livestock. For the local economy, waterway transportation was perhaps most important for moving logs and lumber: around 1913, Portland emerged as the lumber shipping and manufacturing center of the world. Back then, the boats transported the logs and lumber directly from the timber port to their final destinations, usually a mill or other end user. When it came to boats and trade, Dad could talk your ear off.

Years before Lewis and Clark visited our land, Oregon's lush forests were thought to boast an—almost—unlimited supply of trees. Early in the nineteenth century, the first sawmill was built in the Pacific Northwest, with over 170 sawmills operating by 1873. The lumber was sent to faraway places like China, but many entrepreneurs easily made a bucket of money shipping off timber and fruit to the California Gold Rush miners. In the years since the first mills, we have moved through decades of infamous conflict: made in Oregon versus trade; clear-cut versus thin; framed, often, as jobs versus forests. There is no argument, though, about Oregon's forests themselves: bonanza.

My great-great-grandfather, J.K. Gill—brother of the baby in the bucket, son-in-law of Chloe and William—is mostly remembered for the bookstore bearing his name, which opened in 1871 on downtown Portland's Front Street, surviving for decades to come. Though J.K. had long passed, the bookstore was around when I was a kid in Portland: I remember it, as do many others, as a special spot to look for books, school texts, binders, and worldly office things. I most liked to shop for pens at the J.K. Gills of my day.

Less known is J.K.'s early connection to the newspaper industry, the earliest tie-in to the newspaper industry for Dad. Twenty years after opening his Portland bookstore, J.K. Gill joined *Oregonian* publisher Henry Pittock as an incorporator to establish the Columbia River Paper Company. They chose to locate the mill at LaCamas—now Camas, Washington—where they hoped to avoid the risk of flooding. Their original intention was to supply newsprint for the *Oregonian*, a newspaper still in operation today.

J.K. shared in his daily diary that this venture had been a poor financial choice for him. This great-great-grandfather of mine acknowledged that although the Columbia River Paper Company was profitable, he didn't appear to ever receive much compensation for the services he gave as president of the company. The mill also still operates today after nearly a hundred and twenty years.

Of course, the Oregon Territory's oldest, continuously operated paper mill that opened in 1889—our West Linn Paper Company— sits alongside the Falls, just across the river from the site of Dr. McLoughlin's first mill and Oregon City's recently shuttered Blue Heron Paper Mill. And while the West Linn Paper Company still churns out paper, now specialty coated, the shuttered mill across the river inspires preservationists and designers to strategize to save mill parts and structures, and create a unique glimpse into Oregon's past as part of the Willamette Falls Legacy Project.

Somewhere, I hear Dad. "Hurrah. Hurrah."

THE DOCKS WE knew as kids, other than the marinas, were mostly used for recreational access. The years of our bustling waterway had changed. But even during our childhood years on the river, tugboats moved barges—usually floating logs cabled together— past our house and dock, up the Willamette to the mills in West Linn and Oregon City. There the logs had to be unloaded, as the locks weren't equipped to carry large barges around the Falls. Often due to scheduling demands, the large log rafts might be moored to the banks for a few hours or days, until another tug showed up to move them farther.

And this is where our odd family joke originated. Carp had been introduced to Oregon in 1880, for farm fishing. The log rafts moored on the banks of the Willamette, back in the 1960s, were the perfect place for us kids to fish. And a perfect place to spot carp, those bottom-dwelling suckers. It was an August day, the first day aboard our new motorboat Dad had so proudly named the *DeDe*, when our famous Montgomery-trademarked term, *carp-hold*, was coined. Brother Pat observed Dad's fishing mate hooking a carp on the end of a line, holding it up by its gills.

"Carp-hold!" he shouted. Presto. He likened it to catching a person in the armpit.

From then on, Pat—my career educator and doll deformer—exhibited a strange, and terrorizing, fascination with carp. He would chase us, emitting strange sucking sounds, as all of us protected our armpits. Pat generated mad stories about giant sucking creatures, images inspired by the fish as they sucked on the sides of docks. And the stories and threats continue still as Patrick, now middle-aged, gently terrorizes the next generation of family members.

FOR ME, THE carp nightmares began right after a day of waterskiing. Teenage Captain Pat, allowed to steer the boat a short river section if Andy was also along, veered the boat into a slough of dead carp. I wiped out. Right in the middle of them.

"Pat," I yelled, barely audible. Terrified. Swallowing a mouthful of river as I hit the water, knocking off my recently mastered one-ski, worn over a tennis shoe to fit my foot. Stuck I was, in a slough of stinky suckers.

Pat, in slow motion, slowed the boat, turning back toward me. No words I could hear left his mouth. I am convinced, today, that he shared a private chuckle with the steering wheel. And slowly, ever so slowly, inched the boat over to pull me out. And to this day we have agreed to disagree about just how many carp were in that stinky slough—he claims one, I assert it was a whole school.

EVEN STILL, MY fear of carp wasn't half as bad as what I developed for nutria. Nutria, better known as river rats, were introduced into Oregon as early as 1889, the same year electricity ran from the Willamette Falls to Portland. Trappers hoped nutria would be a suitable replacement to beaver—which were beginning to disappear, no surprise. They continued to be imported until shortly before my birth. At one time, Oregon had more than six hundred fur farmers raising nutria for fur. Some animals escaped and others were released into the wild when the farmers realized there really wasn't a market for their rough pelts. Really now. Would you like a nutria pelt?

Though I didn't know at the time how the descendants of the loose nutria were damaging lands along rivers like the Willamette, I was always fearful they lurked along our gooey banks: for some time, I refused to wade in the muddy shallows near our dock. The couple of times we tried to swim across the river, equipped with life preservers and Mom in WhoWho's *Mudhen* for safety, I refused to wade through muddy muck to proudly stand on the opposite bank. Worse, I imagined nutria climbing the banks at night to capture me from my bedroom, worrying that perhaps I was more inviting to them than my brothers, representing the lone young maiden.

DAD SHARED HIS last boat, the *Walrus 4*, with his brother, Bill. At this point, the senior citizen brothers were living in that Southeast Portland Sellwood neighborhood, Dad and Mom in a condo, and Bill in a houseboat. The *Walrus 4* was Dad's all-time favorite. Designed by the legendary George Calkins, the bartender was designed to withstand challenges presented by rough water like the Northwest's raging Pacific Ocean. Although rising fuel prices made the boat expensive to operate and, in the end, it became difficult for Dad to safely steer into its moorage slip—leaving him with white knuckles like his father—Dad loved captaining elaborately guided tours of his favorite river stretches. Children and grandchildren joined him for these fine river escapades as he steered his beloved boat between the Falls and Portland's dry docks, sometimes traveling all the way down the Columbia River, past Astoria, to fish near Ilwaco, Washington. New hires for the Port of Portland accompanied him in other boats and vehicles in later years, now as a retired consultant, on a tour of

Portland maritime operations they would never forget. And Dad—always one for looking for new river stories—continued to gather content for his regular column in the *Daily Shipping News.*

BUT OF ALL boats, Dad most loved steamboats. They ruled the stories he shared: carrying goods and passengers up and down the Columbia and the Willamette. Oh, to have been a passenger on the early steamboats puffing along the two-thousand-mile long Columbia River! Our Columbia: the river that introduced William and Chloe to the Oregon Territory; the second longest river in the United States. The river our Willamette feeds. The Columbia: of rapids, reefs, bars, and strong currents.

Moving downstream on the Columbia might be fairly easy, but fighting the current to go upstream, through white water and falls, was just about impossible in sailing ships or canoes. Pacific Northwest school children learn about Lewis and Clark's 1805 explorations of the Columbia by canoe. But later, as more people explored and settled in Portland and the Willamette Valley, the need to travel by river increased with river navigation easier than land: steamboats became popular along both the Columbia and Willamette Rivers. Steamboats, propelled by paddle wheels on the side or the stern, were easiest to navigate through the winding rivers and could land just about anywhere.

Sam Gill, late 1800s

And, because of steamboats, Dad loved to share stories about his great-uncle, my great-great-uncle, Sam Gill. In Dad's obituary—which he wrote himself, a journalist to the end—he identified Sam Gill as the one to incite his love of steamboats and rivers. Sam died when Dad was only two. But Sam's stories were told proudly by Daddy Dick: my author grandfather who late in life regretted that he had never been able to pull enough material together to write a book about this brother of his grandfather's. Our own dad pored over everything he could find about this self-educated steamboat engineer. And he, too, wrote about Sam in his own columns.

SAM GILL WAS also a writer. He preserved a world long gone when he published his collection of river stories, *Memories of Busy Steamboat Days*, in the *Portland Bulletin*. He wrote in a looping cursive in his journal, *Odds and Ends*, recounting his career building and engineering more than fifty steamers on our two rivers. Today, Sam's original diary and copies of his articles from the *Bulletin* lie safeguarded in the research library of the Oregon History Museum.

Decades after falling into the wash bucket on the crossing to the Eastern United States, Sam followed our great-great-grandfather, his brother J.K. Gill, to Oregon in 1876. Sam began his steamboat career after being laid off from Albina Iron Work. He jumped at an opportunity to work on the *Hayward* steamboat as a fireman and, eventually, he became a steamboat captain.

In the early years of Sam's career, the *Hayward* steamboat ran from Portland to Astoria on Mondays, Wednesdays, and Fridays, returning to Portland on Tuesdays, Thursdays, and Saturdays. The steamboat fare was fifty cents between terminals on the Washington side, or two dollars and fifty cents for meals on the Oregon route. The run followed the Washington shore, across the bay at Harrington's Point, and down to Astoria. Harrington's Point is the legendary spot where, in 1805, Captain Clark stood and believed he was looking upon the ocean. In fact, Clark and his men were gazing at the lower Columbia River Estuary and Grays Bay, and they still needed to travel another twenty miles before they would reach the Pacific.

Sam wrote about the *Hayward*'s direct competitor, the *Willamette Chief*: the supposed namesake for my grandparents' cruiser—luxurious to us kids, but nothing compared to the steamship. The *Hayward*'s boiler allowed only ninety pounds of pressure, requiring the "skill of an expert demon from Hell" to get enough steam on the gauge. When the two steamers were near each other, the Captain of the *Chief* would stand out on the deck jockeying the crew of the *Hayward*, and the ships would dodge competitively up or down the river, no doubt worrying passengers aboard with this early form of road rage.

"I could see Dave in my mind now," Sam wrote. "Pacing back and forth across the engine room, just a'snarling at the opposition, its owners and all its affairs. Finally, the *Chief* would edge up to the *Hayward*, pass them, and Johnnie Marshall, engineer of the *Chief* standing in the engine room door would give Dave a pleasant wave of the hand!"

Sam's boss, Captain Dave, appreciated the efforts of Sam and his fellow firemen to keep the old kettle boiling. When they arrived in Astoria, they would have to burn the fire out, drop the steam down to zero, and get into the firebox to caulk a few of the leaky tube ends.

When Sam worked on ships later in the nineteenth century, he wrote, "Modern 1877 boatmen know nothing about grief, compared to the boilers of old steamers." Imagine what he'd think about travel today.

The list of the steamers running the Columbia and Willamette is long, and Sam Gill worked on many of them. *Beaver* was a popular steamship name, beginning with the first steamer to arrive in Oregon in 1836, just a year before my great-great-great-grandfather William arrived by ship at Fort Vancouver. The stern-wheeler *Multnomah* was built in Portland in 1855 to run the river stretch from Portland to Oregon City, certainly carrying some of our early relatives. And a bit later, the stern-wheeler *Claire* was built by Portland Shipping Company to tow log rafts and barges from West Linn's Crown Willamette Paper Company—today's West Linn Paper Company— to downtown Portland docks and beyond to the paper company in Camas, Washington.

SAM GILL'S FAVORITE story was about the time he met a famous general. Even before the locks on the Columbia River were built, Sam Gill ran boats up the Columbia and, just like anyone traveling by the river at that time, they had to portage around the

Cascade Rapids. While laying over in The Dalles, General William Sherman, who was heading to Fort Vancouver on a mission for the U.S. government, boarded the steamer along with a noisy party, awaking a napping Sam. General Sherman's apology to Sam, however, led to their meeting, followed by a long chat as they traveled down the river to Fort Vancouver.

My favorite Sam Gill story is not about his usual steamer routes on the Columbia or Lower Willamette but about traveling upriver on the Willamette. This trip took place twenty-odd years after his brother's father-in-law, William Willson, and others formed the early Oregon provincial government. On this trip, Sam's steamer swept past points on the river where half a century later, Dad would oar his leaking rowboat and, decades after that, I wiped out in a slough of carp. Today I can take a ride on the Canby Ferry, for old times' sake, and imagine his crossing that stretch of the river.

On this particular day in the late 1800s, Sam Gill was off work, nursing an injured hand. He was walking down Front Avenue in downtown Portland when the engineer of a Willamette ship came up to him.

"I want you to make a trip to Corvallis and back for me, as I am sick," the engineer said.

Sam held up his hand. "Sorry, but my hand is lame. Boss gave me orders not to work."

So the engineer tracked down Mr. Gates, Sam's boss. "Have no worries," the engineer told Mr. Gates. "My assistant will do all the work."

Mr. Gates agreed that, in that case, the trip would be good for Sam: good for him to get out on the river, and gave his approval.

The next morning when he boarded the ship, Sam noticed that the engineer didn't appear to be a particularly sick man. And then, strangely, the engineer disembarked at Champoeg. Sam didn't think too much about it, and all seemed to be going well on this journey upriver. Until their arrival in Salem: as they were docking, a man suddenly burst onboard, armed with a shotgun. He pointed it at the assistant and crew, the only people in sight.

"Where is the engineer of this boat!" demanded the man demanded.

Sam had come out to look at the water gauge, completely ignorant of the situation developing. One deckhand quickly offered up Sam, yelling, "Here he is!" It became clear that the man with the gun was on a serious errand of vengeance.

Fortunately, another shipmate was paying attention. "No—stop! This man is just a temporary replacement. He is not the man you seek!"

The man with the gun looked perplexed for a few moments and was finally persuaded to leave the boat—lucky for Sam Gill and those who loved him.

UNFORTUNATELY FOR THE steamboat industry, diesel tugs soon entered the mix of waterborne vessels. Tugs were cheaper and used smaller crews, and although they weren't as strong and couldn't tow as fast, they began replacing sternwheelers. Soon, many new ships dotted Oregon's waterways and the discovery of steel, aluminum, and fiberglass spawned bigger and busier shipyards. The Portland Shipbuilding Company was one of the oldest and last-standing wooden shipyards in Oregon, building steamers until 1919. The company stayed active until 1964, the same year we moved to the Willamette, repairing and renting wooden barges. Its original building still stands on Portland's Southwest Nebraska Street where today the site is surrounded by the aerial tram and LEED-certified skyscrapers, and looks out toward the new Tilikum Crossing—a bridge designed to carry only pedestrians, bicycles, and mass transit across the Willamette. Sam Gill would never have imagined what this Willamette shoreline would become in a mere century.

DAD'S MOST FAVORITE steamer was the stern-wheeler *Portland*. Now usually docked near Portland's Tom McCall Waterfront Park, the *Portland* begs curious passersby to wonder about its river history. Most will never know, unless they step onto the old steamer: today, the Oregon Maritime Museum. A working vessel for the Port of Portland for forty-one years, the *Portland*'s sole job was to assist oceangoing vessels in the Portland Harbor. Dad was the president of the museum during its three years of restoration, raising the funds to preserve the steamer into the attraction it is today. And in its tip-top shape, it was decorated and rented out to Warner Brothers in 1993 for the making of the movie *Maverick*.

But more important to us, in the end: on a hot September afternoon in 2014, the steamer *Portland* hosted our family and a hundred others as we remembered Dad. Today, the old boat perches on the Portland waterfront, occasionally taking lucky travelers on a river journey, evoking visions of steamers puffing up and down the Willamette and Columbia in days past. And for me, my mom and my brothers, and our children, it will forever remind us of Dad.

Dad (up top) on Steamer Portland

CHAPTER 11
PIRATES

DURING THE FIRST years of the twentieth century—two generations after Sam Gill engineered steamboats up and down the Columbia—Daddy Dick began his earliest steamer journeys along the Columbia to Astoria and back. Like my daughters and me, many years later, Daddy Dick was just a babe the first time he traveled to the town of Ocean Park on Washington's Long Beach Peninsula. In 1883, Reverend William A. Osborne and a party of ten other men, including our J.K. Gill, formed the Methodist Camp Meeting Association, founding Ocean Park, first as a Methodist revival site, then as a town. In his involvement with this group and introduction to Ocean Park, J.K. Gill planted the roots of our most beloved family tradition.

EIGHT MILES SOUTH of Ocean Park, closer to the mouth of the Columbia, is the town of Long Beach: one of the oldest seaside resorts in Washington State. Back before the automobile, getting to the peninsula was much easier from Portland than from Washington cities because of steamship travel on the Columbia. The Portland elite came, as did fewer numbers of working families, staying in hotels when they could, camping in canvas tents when they couldn't.

To my brothers and me, and to our own kids many decades later, the town of Long Beach has mostly meant a short trip to ride go-carts, buy salt water taffy, and stare at Jake the Alligator Man at Marsh's Free Museum. At the peninsula's northern tip sits Willapa National Wildlife Refuge and, nearby, nestled on the shores of Willapa Bay, the quaint town of Oysterville—known for, well, oysters. Midway between Long Beach and the peninsula's tip lies the town of Ocean Park, bordering Willapa Bay on one side and the Pacific Ocean on the other. It was there, on the Pacific side of Ocean Park, that the Gill family and generations to come found their place, even as others were being separated from theirs.

Although some traders explored this finger-shaped peninsula, they quickly learned that beaver and elk didn't live there, and very few white Americans came to the Long Beach area until the 1860s when farmers began to claim homesteads. Eventually, the wild cranberries that thrive in this coastal climate were discovered and developed into a profitable agricultural crop.

Well before Chloe and William landed in the West, so many American Indians had already died that native groups worried whether any of their people would survive. The first of the diseases, influenza, hit Indian villages near the Columbia in 1750, killing three-quarters of the population near present-day Ilwaco. Decades later, ships and traders brought smallpox, followed by successive waves of fevers, tuberculosis, venereal disease, and scarlet fever. When the fur traders left, the local Chinook Indians agreed to give their lands to the Americans in a treaty—but, as was repeated with tribes throughout the West, Congress did not ratify the treaty. This left the Chinook without a treaty or a reservation, forcing the small numbers who had lived through the deadly diseases to move to the Quinault and Shoalwater Bay reservations farther north in today's Washington State. A brave minority remained on their lands on the river and the bay.

WHEN DADDY DICK was six years old, he developed serious complications from a case of scarlet fever. His Portland family doctor suggested a milder winter in the beach climate might help improve his health, so his mother, Georgia, bundled him up, packed a trunk and several suitcases, and headed to the coast with him. Daddy Dick's baby sister, my great-aunt Nan, was left behind in Portland with her grandma and namesake, Frances Gill. Nan remembered waving goodbye to their father during a trip just a few years later from the deck of this same steamer, the *T.J. Potter*. The *T.J. Potter* was thought to be one of the fastest, most luxurious steamboats in the Pacific Northwest—but on both trips the kids were more concerned with the absence of their father onboard, different from other summer trips to the beach as my proper great-grandfather, William A. Montgomery, both times had to stay back to mind the J.K. Gill Bookstore.

I can see this scene through my great-aunt Nan's written memories: a sad Nan on the deck, crying out to her father. A young deck boy approaching, offering Nan a piece of chewing gum, saying, "Here, kid, take this and shut up." I envision Nan soon after excitedly boarding the ship, enormous to a small girl, early in the morning; climbing the spiral staircase and entering a grand dining room with chandeliers. She would be dressed in her fancy traveling dress, and, finally, settle down to stare out the window at the passing riverbank and rippled Columbia.

Later in the afternoon, the steamer would pass Astoria: the place where fur trapping began in the West after John Jacob Astor formed Fort Astoria. The place made famous and romanticized by Washington Irving and his book *Astoria*, written as early as 1835. Today, the Astoria Column juts 125 feet into the sky, built by the Astor family in 1935 to pay tribute to the town's early history. Visitors climb the spiral stairs and peer out toward the expanse of river and ocean, imagining the travels of two centuries ago.

Soon after, there would be a great rush for everyone to get off the steamer and hop aboard a small train at Megler, Washington— now the north side of the Astoria-Megler Bridge—directly across the Columbia from Astoria. Still hours from their final destination, the train carrying these passengers would crawl along the peninsula, stopping first at Beach Center, followed by Seaview, Long Beach, Breakers, and, finally, the final stop, Nahcotta: short stops in tiny towns. Sometimes, the train would stop at the wee town of Loomis so the conductor could stop at his home for lunch as passengers waited a few extra minutes. When the train finally arrived in Nahcotta, a terrific crowd awaited at the station. The two baggage men jostled about in efforts to get baggage delivered by stagecoach to the appropriate homes, including our family's just down the street in Ocean Park. That winter, Daddy Dick settled in, and years after this sickly winter at the beach as a six-year-old boy, my grandfather never forgot the wild winter storms and raging ocean.

I SPENT MY first Thanksgiving at Ocean Park, almost always a stormy time of year. Our daughter Erin's first Thanksgiving of 1990 was too blustery to even take her, now six weeks old, for her first beach walk. My husband—a man who naturally fit as Dad's fifth son— eagerly adopted this house and our Thanksgiving ritual at the beach as his own. That year, flooding abounded, and we crossed deep puddles

on the local roads and highways as we drove to our cabin. And it
began the routine beach trips for Erin, and a few years later, Emily—
often joining other family—not just during stormy Thanksgiving,
but in wet springs and sometimes warm summers. Our family shared
days filled with treks down to the ocean, hoping low tide would come
in the afternoon to give the sun time to warm water-filled, sandy tide
pools. Creating a wide-open space, sometimes with an expanse that
felt endless, for us to prance between pools. Days full of sandcastles
and wave jumping. And other rainy, cold afternoons with Scrabble
games and books next to the radiating warmth of a fire.

Dad with Andy and Pat, 1959

IN OUR FAMILY, reference to "the beach" has always meant
Ocean Park, Washington, rather than the closer Seaside, Oregon.
Over the years, the demographics of the Long Beach Peninsula
changed as wealthier Portland families began to go to Oregon's ocean
resorts, such as Seaside and Gearhart. And though my grandparents
and their parents may have felt part of that circle, our family had
become forever connected to the Long Beach Peninsula.

In those very early days, the drugstore was a favorite for the soda
fountain: Daddy Dick and Nan bought penny candy as did my
brothers and I many decades later, after walking the short mile to
our favorite store, Jack's. And decades after that, my children, and my
brothers' children, would do the same—although it no longer cost
a penny. The climax of the day in Nan and Daddy Dick's time, as it
is now, was watching the sun set over the ocean. Back then, friends

would meet at the ridge at the end of the day, on a long splintery bench shared by many. For the ritual: the watching of the sunset.

As a young man, Daddy Dick started Ocean Park's first lending library in the local store just across from the railroad station. And although he had completed college at the University of California, Berkeley, he had opted to finish his medical training at University of Oregon Medical School in Portland. That is, until he returned to his hometown—a city he missed—and began to spend even more time in his grandfather's J.K. Gill bookstore. It was then that he imagined a literary life might better match his interests than medicine. With his father serving as the general manager at Gill's, Daddy Dick had a leg up: he could get books for a good price, so he set up his first business venture, renting books to the few families visiting Ocean Park. World War I was just breaking out; it was an uneasy time. Perhaps people buried their heads in books to escape, just as I did as a kid with my less-serious brother troubles.

Though Daddy Dick and WhoWho bought a house close to the town of Ocean Park in 1946, it wasn't until 1950 that WhoWho issued the bold statement: "What is the point of owning a beach house if you can't see the ocean?" True to her determined nature, WhoWho sat down at the kitchen table and drew a picture: a cabin on the ridge between Ocean Park and Klipsen, to be built by her neighbor, Perry Mills. And so they built it. Our *Illahee*—loosely translated from the Chinook word for *earth*. A few rooms, a tiny kitchen, a fireplace. Perry shared a fishing boat with Daddy Dick and a few years later agreed that in exchange for Daddy Dick's share of the boat, he would help build an apartment above the garage to provide a bit of solitude away from noisy grandkids: the tower room, where we would ring a bell at the door to announce our presence for tea time—or just for the fun of it.

Illahee before tower room, ca.1953

This original house my courting parents visited, properly chaperoned by Daddy Dick and WhoWho. I can hear Mom's father warning, "Patty, I don't think it's right for you to go away with this young man." He needed not have worried: Mom was tucked away in one of the two bedrooms, Dad up in the unfinished loft with the squirrels. Of course, Mom still likes to remind us of the necking they did on the dunes—in a picture taken just a few short years later, the two of them look like Deborah Kerr and Burt Lancaster in *Here to Eternity*.

Mom and Dad, 1955

In our beach house today, we have a bunk room furnished with four sets of bunks that came from a navy ship: a bedroom turned into a room for all the kids, once we and our cousins arrived. That's where we always slept when we were kids, other than the nights we joined the sand fleas and itched through the dark hours as we tried to sleep on the beach. We each claimed our usual bunk with the youngest kids lacking seniority to claim an upper bunk: us a family of five kids, often joined by cousins, and later, friends. And then, like now, found us huddled closely together around the fireplace if we happened to visit during the coldest months. No television was ever added to this house: a devout family requirement, filling evenings with reading and games. Creating some contention today are those who use our generous neighbor's Wi-Fi to try to keep up with emails while on vacation. Once my brothers and I added our own children to the mix, we introduced live theater to our program by creating often too-lengthy and inappropriately personal original skits involving most family members. My all-time favorite was the Montgomery rendition of the *Wizard of Oz* with Dad playing a bold and powerful Oz, dressed royally in his indigo dressing gown and an inverted basket on his head.

When I imagine our main room at the beach house, even today, I see Dad sitting comfortably in his brown leather La-Z-Boy chair marked with damage from flying sparks, next to an overbuilt roaring fire, with a hardbound book in his lap. If my grandparents could see the beach today, they would be surprised at how the dunes have accreted over the years from the Columbia's silt deposits, creating a much longer walk between the cabin and the beach. While the land must feel the same, Daddy Dick and WhoWho would be amazed at how many pine trees have grown between our house and the dunes, mostly blocking our view of the ocean from the main house. And they would be shocked by our talk of evacuation planning and the catastrophic earthquake-caused tsunami predicted to strike the peninsula, as occurred five hundred years ago. Predicted to wipe out our beach as we know it.

AS CHLOE AND the missionaries slowly made their way up the Columbia River in 1850, they crossed the Columbia's dangerous bar near today's Astoria. Any romantic notions about crossing the mouth of the great Columbia River were quickly dashed: the bar, three miles wide and six miles long, is known as the Graveyard of the Pacific. In 1792, Sea Captain Robert Gray completed the first recorded crossing by a white person. Captain Gray was a hero of Dad's: he even impersonated the captain two hundred years after his lifetime, telling stories of the captain's crossing of the mighty Columbia for local audiences.

As was the practice, Captain Gray sent the ship's small boat ahead of the vessel to search for the deepest water for safe passage. In an interest to protect goods and people, and out of respect to the legacy of this graveyard, local American Indians, followed later by Hudson Bay Company members, served as the earliest pilots to meet ships and help them cross the bar. These early pilot boats may have been nothing more than oversized canoes, rowed out to meet and guide ships. Since the crossing in 1792, as many as two thousand large ships have sunk in and around the Columbia Bar, where the river's current dissipates into the Pacific Ocean. Sediment moving downriver can cause standing waves as it mixes with the ocean's currents. Some have likened the waves to being hit with a fire hose.

The nearby U.S. Coast Guard Station, Cape Disappointment, is known for operating in some of the roughest sea conditions in the world. Adjacent to the oldest lighthouse in the Pacific Northwest, this station responds to hundreds of rescue calls each year and also operates the National Motor Lifeboat School. In the early 1900s, before today's U.S. Coast Guard, the service was called the U.S. Life Saving Service. My great-great-aunts watched these heroes—no women then— stationed at Klipsan; impressed by the daring young fellows who steered their boats out over the breakers near the Columbia Bar. The Columbia River Bar Pilots was established in 1846, and these days, highly trained Bar Pilots guide ships across the bar, often boarding by helicopter just for the bar crossing. The pilot boats of today are all-weather, high-speed craft with full ability to handle rollovers—a far cry from oversized canoes.

Gill family gathering, Klipsan, Washington, 1905

Dad made his last Columbia Bar crossing at the helm of his *Walrus 4* in 1987. On this trip, he was caught in an unexpected storm on an ebb tide and was lucky to make it back to Astoria in his old boat. After that, Dad's stories of our brave Columbia River Bar Pilots were laced with even more awe and appreciation.

FERRY SERVICE ACROSS the mouth of the Columbia began in 1926, though inclement weather would often suspend travel. I have vague memories of crossing on the Astoria-Megler Ferry, in the years after the automobile but before the four-point-one-mile-long Astoria-Megler Bridge was completed, today a connector between Astoria, Oregon, and Washington's Long Beach Peninsula. I remember the challenge of Dad's eager, sometimes impatient attempts to devour a bowl of chowder or chili aboard the half-hour crossing and still get back to our car before we reached the other side—and once we almost lost our cat on the ferry! Construction on the bridge, the longest truss bridge in North America, began when I was a baby, and after it was completed, travelers paid $1.50 toll to cross until the end of 1993. At least once as a broke college student, I drove the long way home through Longview, Washington, to cross on the Interstate Bridge, not able to put together a hundred and fifty pennies.

Our travel to the beach in the 1960s was far less dignified and glamorous than that of the steamboat crowd, with five kids, two dogs, and my parents crowded into our artichoke green Buick Sport Wagon. Often, we would pick up dinner at a McDonald's drive-thru on our way out of Portland to eat along the curving route of the Sunset Highway. I don't believe J.K. Gill could have imagined something referred to as a Big Mac, wrapped in greasy paper from a to-go window and drooled over by dirty dogs in the back of a station wagon, as being anything fit to consume. But we loved it. We were going to the beach!

Driving across the Astoria-Megler Bridge in its earliest days, we would tease our brother, Dickie. "Start looking now—only people from Oregon have round heads."

"What?"

"No, really. People from Washington have triangle-shaped heads. Really."

"No. I've never seen a triangle-shaped head before."

"That's just because everyone here is visiting from Oregon. Just keep looking!"

"And people from Idaho have square heads."

"They do not! I haven't seen a square head. They are all circles!"

"Just wait. You haven't been to Idaho."

DAD'S INTEREST IN our seafaring side of the family developed as he grew close to his uncle John Haradon, my great-uncle. Uncle John—who, as a teen, supervised Dad as he cleaned out those railcars on Pop-Ard's Wilsonville farm—sailed four years in the American Merchant Marines, working as a radio operator aboard T2 tankers during World War II. Uncle John's stories instilled sea dreams in Dad. The memory of this uncle's losing battle to the ravages of alcohol also helped spur Dad's own move to recovery decades later.

But Dad also daydreamed about our connection to mariners of much older days, especially when we were at the beach. He didn't seem to care if some of these stories were legend, undocumented. In one of his *Daily Shipping News* columns, Dad wrote about our long-ago ancestor Nathaniel Haradon, the first sailing master aboard the *USS Constitution*, and related to us through our Pop-Ard. More exciting to all of us, though, was the legend of Captain John Haradon, our great-great-great-great-something—or not. This sea captain became the hero of Gloucestershire, England, after murdering pirates who had been marauding nearby towns—a privateer in our roots!

Growing up with all these stories, and living near the river, my brothers and I fantasized about pirates and privateers. When we had a long car trip to Disneyland, the Pirates of the Caribbean became our ultimate destination. But what we *really* dreamed about were treasure chests. As we got older, we learned, enviously, that our riverside cousins had in fact discovered a treasure chest. Not until many years later did we learn that our uncle Bill had masterminded the map and planted the treasure.

And we never forgot it. For finally—and yet other times seeming "just like that"—we were adults. We'd made it through stitches and broken bones and unhappy days as the new kids at school—even through divorce and arrests. And now, we joined forces, united as adult siblings. Adult friends. And finally, we brought to fruition for our children the treasure wish that had never been fulfilled for us.

LOOMIS, THAT TRAIN pit stop in the early 1900s, was also the name of a lake. Loomis Lake was the home of trumpeter swans. A place my grandparents had canoed with us when my siblings and I were tiny tots. Loomis Lake was adjacent to another set of lakes, Lost Lake and Mallard Lake. And home of, my brothers and I told our own children, pirates. It was during our annual summer *Illahee* reunion in 1999 that these cousins—just four girls at that point, the seventh-generation descendants of Chloe and William—learned about the long-ago-buried treasure.

Dickie had now been Rick for years, having taken advantage of a move during elementary school as the perfect opportunity to rename himself. Rick quietly confided to his nieces that he had only just now uncovered an old treasure map. It was yellow and brittle with age, and charred on the edges. The crudely drawn map identified a body of water located right, smack in the middle of a peninsula—a peninsula bound by the Pacific Ocean and Willapa Bay. Together the girls, of the four-to-eight-year-old crowd, used every resource they could scavenge to figure out where this mystical place might be. They were excited and scared, and very much believed in magic.

Our three carloads pulled into the small gravel lot between Lost and Mallard Lakes. The girls didn't flinch when after arriving at this normally vacant site—stretching our brains to imagine how we might cross this vast expanse of water—two trucks with canoe rentals pulled up. Tailing the trucks was our also-grown cousin hauling two additional canoes. Nor did the cousins notice or care that money never actually changed hands. Not on-site. Patrick, the family sailor, led the way, directing our group of fifteen to parcel ourselves into the four boats, and off we went across the water.

WE SPEAK IN low voices, suggesting pirates and treasure: "Keep an eye out! Use your eagle eyes to let us know if you see anything suspicious! They may be returning for it!" Holding the map and following its directions, Patrick leads us to the far side of Mallard Lake where we dock our canoes in the gooey mud, cautiously extracting our feet as we try to minimize the sucking sounds. We silently creep along a game trail to what we hope will be our destination. To the X that marks the spot. We can almost hear the heartbeats of the excited, but now scared, cousins. We creep along the trail to a muddy bog and one of the girls spots it—a bottle with a note inside, stuck into a tree overhanging the bog. Together my siblings and I hold the cousins and wade into the swamp. The youngest cousin, Cecily, finally reaches the bottle, grabs it, and holds it tightly to her chest. We hustle back to the shore.

Mallard Lake, Long Beach Peninsula, 1999

"Stand back!" Patrick demands. He and Erin—each generation's eldest—carefully break open the bottle and gingerly pull out a map, brittle with age. Another map, marked with an X.

"Maybe a treasure!" the cousins whisper excitedly, nervously, while keeping a lookout for competing treasure seekers.

"Maybe they have knives!" Too many stories told to this young crew.

One of the girls helps interpret the map, assuring us the treasure must be back near *Illahee*.

We paddle again, more energy in our strokes. We arrive back at the cars, return the canoes, and drive the few miles home to *Illahee*. To Dad. Pops. The guy, who even the cousins know, is most knowledgeable about all things history and pirate. And although as these grandkids got older, their Pops openly shared his life lessons and helped them understand what he had learned the very hardest way, I am thankful that all of their memories of him are about the man he became.

We storm into the house.

Dad places a finger to mark his page in his book, sits forward just a little in his La-Z-Boy chair, and begins reciting his oft-repeated stories about Captain John Haradon, wondering aloud what treasures he may have made away with all those years ago. He warns his wide-eyed grandchildren, raising his own expressive white eyebrows, "Others may very well be seeking these exact treasures! We must be very, very careful."

Dad (Pops) and Erin

Dad groans and lifts himself out of his chair, and stiff-kneed, with choppy steps, leads us down our path, through the dunes toward the ocean—toward where he calculates the X to be. Erin, terrified at the possibility of others finding us, nervously watches her strong uncles digging deep into the dunes. And suddenly, the shovel thumps on something hard! Excitement breaks loose! No time to spare! Hearts pound, and eyes squint along the horizon for intruders. A padlocked chest emerges from the pit in the dunes, but we can't open it here—it is too exposed. The cousins giggle nervously as we speed back to the safety of our deck.

Patrick finds a tool to break the lock on the treasure.

"Stand back!" Pops says. "Who knows what might spew out of there! This box has been hidden for generations." He makes a face at the thought of stinky, poisonous gases, holding the disgusted grimace extra-long for the cousins' benefit. Pops puts in a good struggle with the box. He warns his kids and grandkids, "I've seen this before. Don't get your hopes up," as he fails to open the lock. But suddenly, voila! No gases. Jewels and treasures—ruled genuine by the girls. Rings, bracelets, necklaces, trinkets, goblets. The Haradon Family Treasures! The cousins take out each little treasure, one by one, admiring each as a valuable antique. We decide together this chest must forever stay at *Illahee*. Where it sits today. Awaiting another generation to learn its story.

Cousins and treasures

The girls all believed the story for one year, until someone spilled the beans. Emily cried when she found out. Now—sixteen years later—she still remembers the crushing moment when she learned that the treasures came not from Captain Haradon, but from the local Red, White & Blue Thrift Store.

DAD DIED A week before the annual *Illahee* reunion of 2014. We spread some of his ashes in the dunes at sunset, leaving a handful for his brother, Bill, to strew in Mcleay Park. The glowing sunset: the end of time in today's world, unsure of what tomorrow might bring. Each child and grandchild and Mom, pacing the expanse of land between the cabin and the ocean, sprinkling dust and tears. Delivering some of his body back to the land that taught him—taught us all— gratefulness, and how to return.

We return with our children to build sandcastles and play games of Kick the Can, just as darkness falls. The cousins—the girls now in their twenties, though two younger boys have joined the ranks—still beg us to play after dinner. A four-to-sixty-plus age range: sprinting through the bushes and taunting base stickers. "Base sticker base sticker you are a base sticker!" Those of us in jail chant, over and over, jumping and twirling like the strangest cheer squad; awaiting the kick to set us free.

CHAPTER 12
GIRL IN A BOYS' WORLD

WHEN I WAS seven, an eleven-year-old girl from our neighborhood died after falling from a cable crossing tower along the riverbank. This crossing tower was used by the U.S. Geological Service for measuring water depth and sometimes water quality. For the first time, we kids learned that awful things can happen to really nice kids. And we understood, also perhaps for the first time, that any one of us taking risks as we might while exploring and playing, could have been the one to have suffered such an accident.

The houses in our neighborhood were spaced far apart, but there were only nine of them, including ours. We neighborhood kids were close: we had few options for playmates when we tired of our siblings. Her family rebounded by turning memories of a bright, kind, and beautiful daughter into goodness. And as is the way in small communities, lives tightly interwoven yet deliberately private, every parent mourned for the girl. And then, late at night, delivered kisses to the foreheads of their own precious children, thinking, *Thank God it wasn't us. This time.*

THE WILSONVILLE SCHOOL of the 1960s included eight grades, mostly with twenty kids per grade. Each class lined up platoon-style to walk its halls—one line for boys and another for girls; shortest to follow the teacher, tallest in the rear. I always followed directly after each teacher. We each knew exactly who was shortest or tallest and memorized year after year where our place was, happy when a new kid moved in to shake things up. No anonymity in our school. Not only was our bus driver, Cap Kruse, also the custodian and jack-of-just-about-any-trade, his kids were our friends. Most of the lunch ladies, and yes, they were only women, were our friends' mothers. We knew their eagle eyes could capture and communicate a host of messages to our parents, the principal, our teachers and—perhaps worst of all—our friends. If we had older siblings, more than half of our reputation was based on the choices they'd made. There was no hiding within the walls of that school, or the one grocery store, for better or worse.

OUR CHILDHOOD WORLD was white, like other small Oregon towns of the 1960s. In 1968 Wilsonville, Mom went out of her way to find me a playdate of color, inviting over a child of the only black family in our town. A boy she hoped she could recruit into her not-yet public kindergarten class. A family with, yes, you guessed it. All boys.

Why in the world, I asked myself then, *would Mom invite another boy to play with me?* I had boys running out my ears. And this boy was almost two years younger—as if I needed another young boy to hang out with! *If you had to add another to the mix, at least choose one of the boy's older brothers.* In school I had discovered an interest in boys older than me, not realizing then that I didn't feel the need to compete with them as I did with those in my own class. The boys two or three grades older who, while waiting for lunch, lined up around the gym as we younger kids had recess. The boys who I occasionally proved wrong as they bet me a quarter that I couldn't shoot a basketball through the hoop from the corner baseline.

I was good at developing crushes on these boys, my older brothers' friends and fellow scout troop members, following in my earliest footsteps of flirting with the uniformed Babe Ruth baseball players Dad coached when I was a small tot. Andy and Pat teased me mercilessly about this. They fabricated one story, teasing me for decades afterward. The summer we bred our Airedale, we kids sat hushed in the darkened woodshed, watching Colleen deliver her puppies. An early sex-education lesson. Nine of them! The pups' father, our grandparents' dog, Kevin.

Shortly after, Pat accused me. "I can't believe you kissed Mark in the woodshed."

"I did not," I said, my voice raised half an octave and up fifty decibels.

"Yes, you did. It was dark, and you kissed him. He told me about it."

"Why would I kiss your stupid friend? He's not even cute."

"Yeah, that's a good question. Maybe watching the dogs being born." He smirked. "I don't know. You just did."

"You are such a liar," I yelled. The start of another memory still disputed as adults, today.

But back to Mom's attempt to integrate people of color into my life: this boy and I had little in common for a peer-on-peer playdate. I didn't understand at the time what she was doing—nor did Dad—and what I saw was just *another boy* in my life. We made it through the playdate, my younger brothers joining us, with the three boys having a terrific time. Me, muttering. And he did enroll in Mom's kindergarten class: a private kindergarten held across the street from Wilsonville Elementary in the Methodist church; today yet another McMenamins Brew Pub.

While Dad shared childhood stories about befriending immigrant kids at Chapman Elementary School—mostly white kids who came from Western and Eastern Europe—our Mom grew up on Portland's Eastside, graduating from Jefferson High following the creation of Vanport. In Mom's early years, World War II began to change race in Oregon when Portland became the center of the shipbuilding industry with two Kaiser shipyards: Oregon Shipbuilding Company and the Swan Island Shipyard. Shipyard workers were recruited from all over, and the new hastily built city Vanport was constructed on a Columbia River floodplain—destroyed by raging flood waters only six years later—to house wartime workers, with about a quarter of them black. Mom was good friends with a black boy who was on the student council with her at Jefferson High: one of her most favorite boys in all of high school. Dating, though, was a color barrier she didn't imagine breaking back in those days of the 1950s.

I didn't live as a racial minority in a neighborhood until I was in my midtwenties and living in Seattle. In my room for rent during graduate school, on Sunday mornings I would awaken, my second-story bedroom window opened wide to morning hallelujahs from New Hope Baptist Church two doors away. To me, having never lived in a place busier than Portland, the loudness of urban life, downtown Seattle so near, was exciting and foreign. And often exhausting. As I walked back and forth from my bus stop, somedays I didn't see other whites. I didn't expect that I would notice this; that it would feel different. I was bothered that I wasn't color-blind like I expected.

I LIVED A tomboy childhood. I was eager to wear my brothers' hand-me-down clothes and join in their play. In addition to eyeing baseball uniforms, I particularly coveted their navy-blue serge jackets—never finding anything as special in the J.C. Penney girls department. Though I didn't mind opportunities to dress what was then considered "girl-like" on special occasions, I was frustrated at the requirements unique to girls. Such as when we memorized the fifty state capitol names in fifth grade with our teacher, Mrs. Young. Our reward for completing this rote memorization was a Hawaiian Day class celebration where girls were encouraged to track down or fabricate grass skirts and then forced to perform the hula to "Tiny Bubbles." I have no idea what carrot was used to persuade the boys to attend Hawaiian Day, other than being allowed to watch us girls ridiculously attempt the hula.

MY MOM FORMED a Camp Fire troop and assigned herself as the leader just to allow me to have more time with girlfriends. Although they were all girls from my own class, now I got to see them some after school, too, to share snacks and attempt to be crafty— which I wasn't. We made very 1960s kinds of things, like tile ashtrays and painted fabric squares, and somedays earned money to send to a Korean orphan girl named Kim who we sponsored, often meeting in the Methodist church where Mom taught kindergarten. And once when we were really lucky, we walked after school to famed local author Walt Morey's house, where we would sit on the floor and listen to him read from his novel, *Gentle Ben*.

We were all Blue Birds first, then submitted to a ceremony to "fly up" to become full-fledged Camp Fire Girls with the terrible opportunity to sell Camp Fire candy. We competed to sell enough boxes to get a free pass to weeklong overnight camp at Camp Onahlee in nearby Molalla, perched next to the Molalla River. This was no simple feat in a small town, though our neighbors often preferred buying candy to the annual school magazine drive. I was lucky— my friend Suzanne's mom worked at our only restaurant, the Kopper Kitchen. During candy-selling season, Suzanne and I were allowed to stop by after school to share a free chocolate milkshake, made with real hard ice cream in the tall metal mixing cups, and then sell candy in the lobby, giving our neighbors a rest at the expense of the out-of-town and passing-through crowd. And I made it to overnight camp several summers. One night my first year, I wet my favorite Peter Pan pajamas—I remember washing them out in the shared washroom in the morning. Another summer, I developed a huge crush on a counselor named Jenna who wore Levi's and a muted tunic with flowers, had long flowing hair, and sang "Leaving on a Jet Plane" as she accompanied herself on guitar at our nighttime bonfire next to the bubbling Molalla River.

Early on, my friend Suzanne was my connection to all things monetary. Though I grew up with dollars and quarters and chores that sometimes brought in change, when I was nine, Oregon's revolutionary bottle bill went into effect.

"Wanna come over after school today?" she asked me one day. Arrangements were easy back then. Latchkey kids somedays, I told my little brother at recess I wouldn't be coming home on the bus. Somehow we got the messages to our moms without any technology at all. Suzanne lived not a quarter mile from our school, right in the hub of Wilsonville's, then tiny, commercial area. She had two older brothers, so we had similar gripes and needs.

"I wish Mrs. Nelson hadn't left to have a baby," I said. "I really miss her."

"Yeah."

Mrs. Nelson was the buffer between me and the fourth-grade boys I fought with. Two boys in particular: Mark and Craig. I competed hard against them on the kickball diamond. They teased me and I fought back. Mrs. Nelson told me sometimes boys did this when they liked you, but didn't know a better way to act—nobody had ever told me this before. And Mrs. Nelson was our coolest teacher yet: she introduced us to "Feelin' Groovy" by Simon and Garfunkel, a song we were allowed to sing and dance to during the school music concert. It was the same year my parents were separated for three months, with Dad taking an apartment back in Portland. A tough year.

We let ourselves into the back door of Suzanne's house, tossed down our coats, and grabbed an apple. Sometimes we didn't really know what to do when we actually got to play together, both used to flying solo when we tired of playing with boys. This day we went outside. Suzanne had the only monkey puzzle tree I had ever seen, in her front yard. Some say this species of tree, native to Chile, was brought over during the 1905 Lewis and Clark Exposition—the same fair Daddy Dick had marveled at as a child in Northwest Portland. Suzanne taught me how to pull my hand down the branches of the tree the right direction, to keep its sharp claws from biting me.

Next door to Suzanne's house, past a boundary of bushes, was the Silverleaf Tavern.

"Let's get some candy," she said.

At first, I was confused—I had almost forgotten the newest opportunity to earn pennies for candy. And then I remembered. At that point, I was only starting to realize that the Silverleaf was a place that sometimes kept Dad away from us at night, though I did remember seeing beer bottles left in the bushes around its parking lot—this new bottle bill not yet preventing littering. Suzanne and I imagined we were the first kids to act on this mother lode.

"I'll get a bag," she yelled, while I started to troll the bushes. No worries about germs or cuts, we pulled out a dozen or so brown Budweiser and Olympia bottles.

"That's enough for today," she yelled as I kept scouring the bushes, adding more to our treasure trove.

Finally, I followed her across the two-lane Wilsonville Road to our town's one grocery store, no traffic coming from either direction. We proudly hoisted the bottles up to Mr. Lowrie at the till. He met us with his friendly hello and a penny for each bottle.

"How's your mom and dad?" he asked me.

"Good," I said quietly. Family problems: private business.

Suzanne whispered, "I'd rather get the candy at the gas station." So we tromped across the street again, to the penny-candy dispenser at the Shell Station.

IT WASN'T UNTIL I was ten that I began to really notice serious differences for girls in the outside world. Up until then, I had complained about relatively petty things being unfair for me as compared to boys. But it wasn't until news spread that a local teenage girl was raped in a nearby holly orchard that I understood that especially bad things can happen to women. Before that, I didn't pay attention to stranger danger, or think it any riskier for me to walk down a street alone than it was for my brothers.

This rape divided our community—some said the girl made it up, others feared an outsider had come in to destroy our quiet, protected world. Because my brothers had activities keeping them after school or rode a different bus shift, I was immediately impacted. The school prohibited Cap from dropping me, and any other girls in situations like mine, alone at the bus stop, nearly three-quarters of a mile from our home. This was quite a distance: when we were running late in the morning, we'd ride our bikes to the bus stop, then ditch them in the bushes.

Now, Cap was to drive down the steep hill of Rose Lane and drop me near the birch trees at the end of Montgomery Way so I could avoid walking alone on the deserted stretch, and instead pass just a few homes on my shorter journey to our doorstep. Rather than feeling safer or happier to have a shorter walk, I was angry—a new kind of angry I hadn't known before. To lose my freedom because I was a girl! This escalated the unfairness of all the other little things I had observed in my short life, like not being allowed to play Little League and consistently being assigned the chore of cleaning bathrooms.

Sometime later, the community learned that the local sex offender threat no longer existed—although I didn't know exactly why. But I became oddly hypervigilant. From then on, if I spotted a car coming from afar while walking alone on our street, I would hide in the bushes until danger passed. Hiding behind the scotch broom—bare in the winter, scratchy yellow blossoms in the late spring—I began a new obsessive practice of finger tapping. I had recently begun after-school typing classes—an odd choice for a ten-year-old, typing—to mimic Dad's own fingers as he wrote his stories. Now, in response to this fear I didn't understand, I moved my fingers in the air from behind the bushes, typing the letters on the license plate of the car that had passed. I would repeat the pattern of keystrokes three times, my lucky number. And then I would breathe a sigh of relief, believing this act would keep me safe. Occasionally, half a century later, I still notice my fingers moving.

Moving into our final couple of years living on the banks of the Willamette, although sounds still came from Dad's typewriter, especially late into our weekend afternoons and evenings, I knew that something was amiss, although I still offered tips to his shouted-out queries: How do you spell perceive? Does annoyance have two n's? And he did still find a dictionary in me, a temporary solution to dyslexia as he was living in our house again—and commuting to Salem for work, having left advertising, an industry he never liked much. Although he was happy to get out, the politics of working for the attorney general had its own unique stressors. Though Dad was still always there for our weekend river adventures, I began to see things differently.

TODAY WE LOVE to watch the movie *A Christmas Story* as winter holidays near. What draws us most to this story is Ralphie's mother's fear that he will shoot his eye out if he receives the BB gun he so covets. Unlike many Oregon families, we weren't a hunting family. But we had BB guns, begged for by my older brothers. Imitating them, my little brothers and I would tromp off with one or the other gun in hand to the woods to attempt our own target practice. We would grab a few green bean and tomato cans out of the garbage, no recycling bins in those days, rip off the paper labels, and carry them along with the guns to our fort in the woods. There we would line up the cans on a log and each try to "ping" one, knocking it off the log. I soon tired of this practice and am afraid to imagine what my brothers did when not under the usually watchful eyes of their older sister.

But Ralphie's mom really did know about guns and boys, perhaps like Ralphie, and definitely like brother Andy. He was out one day with friends doing who knows what. Mom got a call from the mother of his friend David.

"Andy has gotten a stick poked in his eye and needs immediate attention," she nervously said.

We made another trip to nearby Oregon City, this time to visit a college friend of Dad's, his eye clinic up at the top of the hill near the Oregon City elevator. As Dr. Campbell tended to Andrew's eye, his concerned expression reconfigured to include tinges of suspicion.

"Awful lucky not to be blinded, Andrew," he said.

"Yeah," Andy stammered. "I'll be okay, right?"

"Mostly okay. Might lose a little peripheral vision on that side. You know what that means?"

"Um . . . yeah, I guess so."

"Hmm, a stick, eh?" asked the doctor asked.

No reply from the kid in the doghouse.

"Sure looks a lot like it could have come from something else. You sure about that stick?" the good doctor asked again.

A long silence. "Um . . . yeah, I guess so," he repeated.

"Well, just in case. You be careful with those BB guns. They aren't toys, you know. And you could lose your eye," he added.

"Yes, Dr. Campbell," Andrew said, barely audible, as the doctor patched up the eye.

Many years later, Andy admitted to Mom that he, David, and their friends were actually shooting each other—a stupidly common practice—aiming for the shoes or ankles, when someone misfired. Although I have never understood the popularity of paint-balling half a century later, it was probably created by grown-up kids like Andy. Ralphie's mother really was right to worry.

That story was topped just a year later by brother, Mike. Just after dinner, Mom made a trip into the living room, our grand room with plate glass floor-to-ceiling windows looking out to the deck and beyond the river. The pride of our home. River view.

I heard Mom say loudly, "What the . . . ?" And a long silence.

Dickie and I followed her into the living room. She was staring, dumbfounded, mouth slightly agape, eyes fixed on a point about four feet up the window. She looked at us. "Can someone tell me why there is Scotch Tape on the window?" She went over to the window and removed several layers of Scotch Tape, leaving one piece still stuck, cemented by the warmth of the afternoon sun. And under that, a layer of aluminum foil.

"Uh-oh," Dickie said, looking at me.

Mom peeled off the foil and the tape, leaving a sticky adhesive trail. Clearly outlined under this final layer of tape and foil was an extraordinarily small, round hole—made only by one thing we can imagine. Mom looked at me and Dickie and shrugged. Her eyes penetrating question marks. We noticed that Mike suddenly had disappeared. Our mischievous brother who two years after falling asleep on the trailside log, hid Dad's prized pipes, before he gave up smoking. The last missing pipe eventually found in a toilet.

"Michael!" my mom called.

Mike sheepishly slinked in, having been listening around the corner. "How could you tell?"

A new rule was created. No BB guns in the house.

CHAPTER 13
CHAMPOEG

AS A KID, my favorite boating destination was Champoeg Park. Mom would pack a no-nonsense lunch, we'd don swimsuits, shorts, and sweatshirts and clamber down the riverbank—running down the stairs and ramp to the dock where we would pile into the *DeDe*. And upriver we'd go, the outboard engine ringing in our ears and my hair flying in the breeze as our wake created waves to splash against neighboring docks.

Once we made it south of Boones Landing, Dad would slow the boat: he always took this stretch extra slow. He really was at his best with us on the river, steering while joking with us and thinking of his own young days: a leaking rowboat and soda pop. Some trips we would stop off at Homer's Marina for gas. And then, finally, we'd arrive.

Dad and whichever kid was closest would tie the lines up to the cleats on the edge of the dock at Champoeg, and we would climb ashore to explore the riverbanks—cottonwoods and river water seeping through our pores. We would dash up and down the dirt paths along the riverbank, some days playing hide-and-seek. This spot was perfectly located on the river between Oregon City, often called the Falls, and Salem—between Oregon's first city and its eventual capitol—and could be accessed by land or water. Champoeg's rich, fertile land, long home to American Indians, attracted white people: people who converted the Kalapuyan word for edible root, *yampa*, into *Champoeg*. Champoeg was the site of the first Hudson Bay Company warehouse on the Willamette River, and was the shipping point of the first wheat in our valley as early as 1830.

Our William Willson stood on this same bank, appointed by his peers as one of three secretaries during Oregon's famed May 2, 1843 meeting. On this day, William joined forty-one other men to vote in support of a provincial government. While I grew up believing the vote was to decide that Oregon Country should be owned by the United States rather than the United Kingdom, in actuality the question to be voted on was whether or not "to organize themselves into a civil community and provide themselves with protection." This meeting following the series of "Wolf Meetings," to figure out how to keep wolves—and bears, panthers, and other animals preying on livestock—out of the settlers' way. The May 2nd meeting came on the heels of the Oregon Memorial of 1838: a written statement claiming the value of the Oregon Country and urging the U.S. Congress to assert its right over the region. Every member of the Methodist Mission, and others, signed this statement—nearly all white men in the Territory then, including William. This statement—really a petition—traveled in a little trunk strapped to Dr. Jason Lee's horse as he rode by horseback from Oregon to the Missouri frontier, then across lakes, along canals, and overland by stagecoach to Washington, D.C. The petition identified potential future commerce with the Orient and South and Central America, making the case that California was landlocked at its Golden Gate as a Mexican province: it was the Oregon Territory that looked out to the Pacific. Settlers and missionaries requested that Congress enact a law in the Territory to protect and control American citizens: to support the "germ" of a great state. All of it, right or wrong, is part of our state's history. Our home's history.

Back on the famous day of the signing, over a hundred years before my birth, settlers came to Champoeg from all directions and by all means: boats cruising along the river, horses wading across streams and riding over plains. Old and young—mountain ranger, missionary, seaman, blacksmith, merchant, doctor, farmer. Pioneers who had, for all kinds of reasons, given up the life they had led somewhere else to imagine a new future. The gathering crowd was too large for any existing building, so the meeting was held on high ground right on the bank of the Willamette—right where my tennis-shoed feet frolicked so many years later.

On that day, William and others voted to proceed with a provisional government or organization for protection and to be secured under law and order among themselves until such time that they would follow within jurisdiction under the American flag. At least one source reports that the first vote was defeated, but the revote led to a final decision carried in favor by two votes. In the end, two Canadians voted with the others to secure the vote for these soon-to-be early Americans. Yet another strike of several to prevent Dr. John from securing this beautiful territory for England. Although I didn't understand all the details, it seemed impossible to us kids then that England, a land so foreign and far away, might have owned our homeland.

As a kid, I would scramble up from the dirt trails below to find my brothers hidden deep in bushes, or even a bathroom when a tree wouldn't do. From the boat dock at river's edge up to the monument, we barely slowed down—except when Dad was nearby to point out, again, the spot where William's name was etched, along with forty-one others, on the monument overlooking the river. A monument crafted and dedicated years after the signing, in 1901. Soon after the vote for the provisional government, more settlers—primarily white—filled up the Territory: Oregon Fever had begun.

Monument at Champoeg

Our ugly racial discrimination continued. Oregon's new leaders, for a short time, adopted a black exclusion law: during Chloe and William's time, it was legal to publicly whip any black person attempting to settle in Oregon. The Oregon constitution of 1857 banned slavery, but made it illegal for blacks to own property, make contracts, vote, or use the legal system. Even when legally allowed, many blacks who could afford to emigrate westward found it a better choice to live somewhere other than our state, making both California and Washington more diverse early on, creating early roots leading to decades of racial inequity in Oregon, still visible today.

The town of Champoeg prospered and grew through the 1850s, boasting a ferry crossing on the Willamette and a stagecoach office—until disaster struck in 1861. Following a wet fall, a winter weather system dropped rain on the Willamette Valley for eighteen straight days. When the Willamette River crested it was as much as thirty feet deep on the Champoeg bottomland, flooding the town and destroying most everything. Nobody lived there again until 1880, when the town reestablished itself nearby as Butteville, the closest town to where Dad took his rowboat on his earliest solo adventures on the Willamette.

THE DAY AFTER Dad died, we knew where we needed to go. We had spent long hours in the hospital—a hospital just above the floodplain of the Tualatin River. We had held his hands; watched him take his last breath as the hour approached midnight; watched the lights flash in his room, unexplainably, immediately after he left us. I had removed his jade wedding ring from his still-warm hand without asking my brothers, giving it a new, permanent home on my own middle finger of my right hand.

Though a Willamette Valley July drizzle had persisted that day at the hospital, the sun broke the next morning. We walked along the trail near the river at Champoeg, some of it now paved, the dips and valleys still etched in our muscles. Laughing one moment with a shared memory of a goofy story, crying the next. Quiet for some time after. It was still so difficult to reckon that this man—this living Oregon history encyclopedia—had left us. Like so many fathers before him. The warm July sun dappled through dense cottonwood leaves, softening the darkness, defusing a barely perceptible amount of the despair that had overwhelmed me the night before in the stark hospital room. Melting edges of a numbing disbelief.

My cell phone rang as I rested with Mom on a bench next to the monument. An unknown number at the other end: Dad's cardiologist, calling to share his condolences. To tell me how much he liked Dad. How he had hoped Dad could have made it to his eighty-fifth, but that his heart was too worn out.

"You were his favorite heart doctor," I told him. Thanking him. I shared with him how—following his last medical exam—Dad had repeatedly laughed about how much he had enjoyed the reference this doctor made about the doctor Dad "fired" after he made inappropriate comments about Dad's heart infection. Dad just couldn't believe that a formal, polite doctor would refer to another in such a way. And he had laughed.

I felt full to be in this place where generations of family once walked: to be in one of Dad's favorite places. Yet I felt so empty. Empty that the storyteller and memory holder was gone. I hadn't asked enough questions. I hadn't listened close enough. I wanted one more day. How is it none of us ever really believe this day will come? Later, alone in the shower, I sobbed. Days and weeks after, riding my bike to work along a particular stretch of the Willamette's waterfront, my tears dripped. Morning after morning.

FRAMED ON THE wall inside the Visitor Center at today's Champoeg State Park is a painting that depicts the signing of the provisional government and illustrates the May 2nd gathering attendees: all men, all white. Although the names are labeled nearby, it is easy for me to make out the face of William Willson, husband of Chloe, father of three daughters including my great-great-grandmother Frances. William died before knowing Frances's future husband, his son-in-law, J.K. Gill. In this painting, The Birth of Oregon by Theodore Gegoux, the group is led by Joseph Meek, and William is one of the few men looking outward toward the viewer. William's look stops me in my tracks: as if his expression holds a desire to convey something. To share the stories.

CHAPTER 14
FLOODS, EARTHQUAKES, AND VOLCANOES

WHEN CHLOE AND William moved, separately, up the Columbia River to Fort Vancouver, our Cascade peaks—Mount Hood, Mount St. Helens, and Mount Adams—welcomed them to the volcanic landscape of the West. I can imagine Chloe's outcry:

"Blessed be to God for his creation of snow-capped peaks that tower to the sky!"

On clear days, Chloe and her fellow Methodists may also have seen graceful Mt. Rainier towering to the north, and craggy Mt. Jefferson to the south. I am certain that never would she have imagined, then, that two of her daughters and a son-in-law might climb to the top of Mt. Hood less than a quarter of a century later.

J.K. Gill, Frances, and Kate climb Mt. Hood, 1892

Chloe and William witnessed the same ice cream cone top of Mt. St. Helens that I beheld throughout my childhood. When St. Helens blew her top, in May of 1980, it was something that even the oldest residents of Oregon had never experienced. It had been almost a century before even Chloe and William's time since any volcano had interrupted life along the Willamette Valley. Mt. Hood's last major eruption occurred in the 1790s, not long before Lewis and Clark's expedition. Mt. St. Helen's blast of 1980 was heard hundreds of miles away throughout the Pacific Northwest. The ash cloud was dense enough to screen out nearly all sunlight in the Washington cities of Yakima and Spokane. And even I, a college student living in a dorm in Missoula, Montana, felt the gritty ash blow into the Missoula Valley as I rode my bicycle toward campus one Sunday. Dark clouds pushed from the west into the valley, obscuring the sunny day, stinging eyes. I spent hours frantically trying to call my parents on the dial-up phone on the wall of my dorm.

"If we have this much ash here, what must Portland be like?" I asked my roommate. Not yet understanding the eastward-wind direction of the ash cloud.

Missoulians moved their bandanas from the usual places around foreheads to cover noses and mouths for days before we all were told the silica particles weren't small enough to penetrate our deep lung sacs. Students celebrated: "The university is cancelled all week!"

Dede at Spirit Lake with Mt. St. Helens, 1978

While I learned the next day that friends and family in Portland were fine, I didn't know for a while the damage done to the area around a special family vacation spot, Harmony Falls Lodge on Spirit Lake, and the lives lost in the eruption. Spirit Lake also housed an old YMCA camp where my dad had camped as a boy. Once a peaceful place with a spot-on view of the rounded white top of Mt. St. Helen's, Spirit Lake was now gone. For months following the eruption, the U.S. Army Corps of Engineers managed to deal with the flow of debris into the Toutle, Cowlitz, and Columbia rivers. People looking to make a few bucks sold vials of the ash to passing tourists. The crew of *Dredge Oregon* worked alongside others clearing the Columbia River channel. And Dad, by this time working for his final employer, the Port of Portland, coined a short-lived phrase, stenciled on a few T-shirts: "Cheap Shot Mother Nature."

WHILE VOLCANIC ERUPTIONS occur rarely in the Willamette Valley, large floods are common. River folk know floods. Flooding of property has been a challenge facing the Willamette River's human residents as long as people have inhabited the floodplains: although Native Americans best understood nature's cycles and adjusted their seasonal migration cycles accordingly. Many of us still take chances building on floodplains, ignoring the patterns of natural history. Our own town was established farther up the riverbank after a flood wiped out West Linn's ancestor, Linn City, in 1861, the same winter storms that destroyed Champoeg.

I was too young to remember the Christmas Flood of 1964, a whopper walloping the Pacific Northwest and Northern California. This one-hundred-year flood affected nearly every river and stream, not sparing the Willamette. Seventeen Oregonians died as waters consumed the region, causing hundreds of millions of dollars of damage. Oregon City was flooded by several feet of water, briefly diluting the ferocious beauty of Willamette Falls. The Tualatin and Clackamas Rivers backed up into our Willamette: the water had nowhere to go but up.

Our lonely cluster of homes on the Willamette's steep bank in Wilsonville was spared—our home in the middle of construction, but WhoWho and Daddy Dick fully immersed in life in Wilsonville. But our homes were stranded from the main road with the lower-lying meadow of the not-yet-founded Boone Borough, River City, and my yet-to-be-skated Hans Brinker Pond now flooded, separating us from the higher plateau and road connecting us to town. Legend has it that WhoWho boldly navigated her canoe—or was it a rowboat?—up our road, the now-rippling Montgomery Way.

Floodwaters didn't slow down my live-life-dangerously grandmother. Our grandmother Dorothy was nicknamed by her eldest granddaughter as the soon-to-be "WhoWho" because she would often enter a room with a "hoo hoo" welcome, though Daddy Dick sometimes said it was because she could be nosy. She preferred her red jeep to a sedan, her blue *Driving Miss Daisy* style cap to any fancy bonnet. And certainly sensible shoes to any heels, at least when she wasn't in throne: WhoWho was a 1925 Portland Rose Festival Princess and, twenty-five years later, a Rose Festival Court Chaperone.

WhoWho as Rose Festival Princess, 1925

I imagine as our KGW news station began to forecast the rising river waters, my grandmother wisely left her jeep at the top of steep Rose Lane where it intersected Wilsonville Road. And what of my grandfather? Perhaps WhoWho urged him to get out of the house and get himself to work. "Dick, you really need to get out of that chair and on your merry way."

I imagine him in his study, listening to another album of John McCormack on his record player, unaware that any minute they might lose power. He was a bit of an intellectual who often seemed lost in thought, and though always, always kind, not one to get down on the floor and play with us kids. A hardbound book on his lap, favorite pipe in hand.

Daddy Dick, 1934

My grandmother finally leaving with a quiet huff. "Somebody has to get out and get supplies. We'll both starve waiting for you." Setting out to, somehow, carry or push the canoe from behind the house into the strangely rising waters. Or was it her son, Bill—living now in his boathouse—who came to her rescue, leaving me with a story I have adapted to meet my childhood expectations of my grandmother? It was only a few years later that another raging storm would unleash Bill's boathouse, just recently sold to a neighbor, from the pilings, carrying it downriver through turbulent waters and on over the Willamette Falls.

But during this storm of 1964, I imagine Daddy Dick turning another page in his book, speaking to himself, almost unconsciously, "She is a most remarkable woman." Taking a moment to look away from his page while leaving a finger on the word he was reading, like Dad, reminiscing.

Daddy Dick first saw WhoWho at a party after she was selected as a Portland Rose Festival Princess. She was nineteen, and newly graduated from Portland's St. Helen's Hall. He was ten years her senior. She shared stories of the 1925 Rose Festival Parade, remembering the Jantzen Knitting Mills float; adorned with "brazen" girls wearing bathing suits, protested by the Portland Federation of Women's Clubs.

On their first date, Daddy Dick and WhoWho paddled a canoe on Lake Oswego. And though WhoWho's father, Pop-Ard, thought she was too young to get married and sent her away to California, WhoWho's daily letters to Daddy Dick made her father relent, allowing her to return to Portland. They married eight dates later.

Little did Daddy Dick ever know—as unconventional as WhoWho could be—how tightly she controlled herself in public so as to never embarrass him, the gentleman. This author and radio book reviewer who told his grandkids that our family represented "intelligencia without money." The man with a strange sense of humor, who taught me a new joke every time I visited—most every day.

"DeDe the Wheedie! I've got a new joke for you today," he would say. This nickname I had graduated to after my first few years as DeDe-FooFoo. He renamed me after I took to adding "foofoo" after all of my loved ones' names, including my Grandma Daum, who apparently didn't much appreciate it.

"What is it, Daddy Dick?"

"A man came into the grocery store, he spit on the wall, he spit on the floor, and when he went out, he spit on the door." Chuckling.

"Now, Dick! You clean that up this minute," WhoWho would cut in. "She is your young granddaughter."

"Yes, dear."

I'd look at him. Wishing he would keep treating me not like a young granddaughter.

"How's this?" he'd ask, an eye to WhoWho. "A man went into the grocery store, and when he went out, he slammed the door."

I'd laugh politely. Disappointed.

CHAPTER 15
CHEMEKETA

ONE OF MY earliest most special memories of WhoWho is from a shopping trip to Salem—a trip to buy me a new pair of Mary Janes. And go to lunch. An unusual day: to be alone with my grandmother, no boys hogging her attention. We rode in her red jeep, navigating the still-new Interstate 5. We chatted about things important in the eyes of a five-year-old, and she didn't interrupt me—not even to point out the location, as we crossed Boone Bridge, where her family's Butteville farm had been: where Dad rode his horse, Nick, and loitered along the Willamette.

Later that morning, as I clutched my carefully selected pair of white Buster Brown sandals, we talked about where to go to lunch while we stood at the Meier & Frank shoe department counter in downtown Salem, within blocks of my great-great-great-grandparents' old house and land claim. A Salem that in a few years would be Dad's daily destination for the last year he lived in Wilsonville, to his job working for Oregon's attorney general, Lee Johnson. And Dad would never tire driving that stretch in those days—Wilsonville to Salem—to reach this job, his ticket out of advertising.

SOON AFTER HE voted in favor of Oregon's provincial government in 1843, my great-great-great-grandfather William's body began breaking down. Around the same time, the Board of Missions was finding fault with Reverend Jason Lee's fiscal management, record keeping, and basic missionary results, eventually replacing him. Over time the new leader, Reverend George Gary, tried to stem the financial loss of the Methodist Missions by giving laypeople the choice of remaining in Oregon or returning to the East. In the end, most laypersons and clergy chose the West. By late spring of 1844, Chloe and William were asked to move from Oregon City to Chemeketa

Plains where William was to serve as an itinerant preacher and Chloe was chosen to open the new Oregon Institute.

By the time Chloe and William left Oregon City, it had grown to a population of close to three hundred-plus people: a town with three sawmills, two grist mills, stores, a school and two churches, and even a public library. The Methodist missionaries imagined that a team of itinerant preachers would travel the Willamette Valley and the Umpqua settlement of Southern Oregon to support the scattered settlers. And in this change from original missions, these were to serve settlers rather than to continue the unsuccessful attempts to convert Native Americans, although California's "gold fever" ultimately reduced those who might be served. William also figured that the rudimentary medical skills he had learned onboard as he sailed around the horn would be useful in Chemeketa, a name given by our Native Americans—the Kalapuyans—meaning "meeting or resting place," and pronounced "Chim-i-ki-ti."

After the Methodist Mission moved to Chemeketa, it was often known as the Mill due to its location near Mill Creek. And although William would do some preaching, and regardless of how much medical knowledge he actually held, he believed he could support his family and save the struggling missionary society money by moving upriver and working in the growing town.

As William and Chloe made this decision, Chloe was torn between her desire to convert Indians and her ever-present fear of violence. She worried that many would consider their leaving the Falls a failure. I can't fully understand the importance she placed on her original mission, nor can I—through today's lens—empathize with the disappointment she felt in their failure to convert American Indians to Christianity. Chloe felt she had failed at what she'd identified as her highest purpose. At twenty-one, she was the youngest of the Methodist missionary adults to board the *Lausanne* that day in 1839. The year before, her father had attempted to arrange a wedding with a young man named George. "A good young man who can take excellent care of you." And when Chloe argued vehemently against this, her father added, "Now, Chloe, don't get any fool notions into your head. There's no place in this world for a young woman without a man."

Six weeks before the *Lausanne* departed, Chloe heard the call that would change her life. During a Young Ladies' Class at Greene Street

Mission, Brother Lindsay's call for young women to teach the Indian children of Oregon spoke to her. The American Board of Missions and the Methodist Church were seeking volunteers to take Methodism into the great West. Chloe's sister, Laura—after failing to talk Chloe out of her plans—encouraged their father to allow Chloe to go with the missionaries as far as New York, convinced that Chloe would decide at the last minute not to continue with the voyage, and return instead to her seminary studies at Wilbraham Academy. But Chloe, later referred to as "four feet of greatness," shocked and disappointed Laura and their parents. Chloe confided to her diary shortly before her departure, "I have spent the day in writing to friends whom I never spect to see again on this earth. O that I may meet them in Heaven!"

And then, just a few years later, William and Chloe did call it quits as traditional missionaries, leaving the Willamette Falls for Chemeketa, with Chloe choosing instead to "give a proper direction" to the youth of our country. There, the couple made what historians today identify as their real mark in Oregon history: founding the town of Salem and Willamette University, and referred to over a century later by Willamette University as "Salem's first power couple." The Oregon Institute opened in the fall of 1844 as the first school for white American children—and those with both white and Native American blood—west of Missouri. This Oregon Institute moved into the frame of what was originally the failed Indian Manual Labor School, the structure and the land purchased by the missionaries for $4,000 for this new enterprise: to teach white children. William kept busy, often many miles from the plains of Chemeketa, as both a preacher and medical provider. And though missing William, Chloe remained busy with her scholars, many who boarded in the school, requiring Chloe to not just be president, dean, and registrar, but foster mother as well.

Chloe was the first teacher, and began with only five students, mostly children of the missionaries. Eventually, she added a few "young ladies from the Falls" as borders to her class roster: the girls would catch steamers at the Falls and arrive at Salem's Wheatland Landing. This same building was used to house the first session of the legislature to meet in Salem along with the first United States court. At a mission meeting, it was determined to use Feb. 1, 1842, as the founding date for Willamette University, creating some contention as to whether it was the first university in the West, west of the Rockies, or west of the Missouri.

Regardless, Willamette University was one of the first coed universities in the United States, and its first graduate, Emily York, a woman. In its earliest years, Willamette University designed the selling of "perpetual scholarships"—$500 cash or cash plus livestock or other resources to assist financing this school. Both Chloe and William purchased perpetual scholarships, imagining that their heirs for generations would have tuition prepaid, never conceiving of a time that this scholarship plan would not keep up with the cost of higher education. The scholarship program was long abandoned before me, my siblings, or our cousins might have benefited.

MANY HISTORIANS BELIEVE William was the one to rename Chemeketa as "Salem," triumphing over other proposed names: Woronoco, Multnomah, Corvallis, and even Algebra. He is recognized as the city's founder, filing the first plat of the city and owning the original land occupied by both Willamette University and our state's capitol. The land claim had originally been held by James Olley, but after his drowning on the Willamette and subsequent remarriage of his widow to David Leslie, the Olley claim was assigned to William to hold for the mission. And our Chloe is recognized as the region's first—white—teacher from her days beginning at Nisqually through to the Institute.

Soon after, some of the property owned by the Institute, now Willamette University, was sold to make up what we now know as much of downtown Salem, including our capitol. As more settlers arrived in the west, the Oregon Institute Trustees, which included William, worried that others might "jump" their land claims. As a way to protect the land William held, along with claims Leslie and two other trustees held, they surveyed and filed a plat map, hoping they would be able to sell town lots to help finance the Institute. William filed the map for downtown Salem reaching thirteen blocks by five blocks, a map one can still see at the Willamette University Library Archives. About fifteen families lived in the land area designated for the Oregon Institute. Land decisions that had once been so simple began getting more complex with disputes common, including some involving our William and Chloe.

The school continued to grow, expanding from one classroom, and late in 1846 William built my great-great-great-grandparents' first Salem home on the riverfront, today property owned by Boise Cascade at Front and Ferry/Trade Streets. William continued to travel—both as a preacher, to places like Fort Clatsop and Fort George, as well as a commissary agent throughout the Cayuse War, not to mention trips to Oregon City during the years of his gold mint operations. While more was happening now in Salem, Oregon City continued to be the territorial capitol until 1851.

Chloe and William became parents with the birth of my great-great-grandmother Frances in 1848, and two other daughters within the next few years. William and a partner opened a general merchandise store near the steamboat landing a few years later, then he installed Salem's first drugstore in 1853, where he often entertained friends and patients with stories of his whaling and seagoing adventures from when he was young. Also that year William and Chloe began building a new home on the corner of Court and Capitol Streets. Salem had grown to a town with five hundred settlers. Although there were still worries and difficulties with fighting between settlers and Native Americans in parts of Oregon, and local challenges such as the burning of the capitol, likely caused by arson, the new Oregon seemed shiny to some.

William and Chloe were kept busy with town, church, and Institute activities. But, shortly after selling his drugstore, William suddenly died at age fifty-one, while visiting with another store proprietor. He died laughing, so the story goes, joking with a friend or fellow worker, leaving Chloe with three daughters under the age of ten. Medical aid was procured but to no avail, with the immediate cause of death attributed to congestion of multiple organs: lungs, heart, spleen, and probably brain.

What must my great-great-great-grandmother have felt? Within less than a year, Chloe sold their home, gave her furniture to the Institute, and for the first time since her original departure, made a trip to spend time with relatives back in Connecticut. In contrast to her original westward journey, now she traveled with her three children in tow: by stagecoach over the mountains of California, ship to Panama, train across the Isthmus of Panama, ship again to Boston, and train to Hartford.

It was several years later, in 1863, that Chloe returned to Oregon with her daughters, the growing girls unhappy to leave their new, sophisticated lives in the East. Chloe took on the job of governess of the Ladies Department at Willamette University, similar to dean of women. And she provided lectures to the young women boarding with her, such as one titled "The Sphere of Women." Her daughter, my great-great-grandmother Frances graduated from the Institute with four others just a few years later.

Was it Chloe's love for the wildness of Oregon, her memories of her late husband and his commitment to their land deed, or her desire for her children to live in the West that led her to leave this final time— to return to the West for good? Perhaps her decision to return was precipitated by the arrival of a long envelope of oiled cloth, sealed by red wax: An envelope delivered by mail just a year before she returned in 1862, signed by President Abraham Lincoln. Finally, she received the land claim certificate for land staked jointly in 1850. A certificate William didn't live long enough to see.

Today, it is hard to conceive of a time when land was simply given away. The Donation Land Claim Act encouraged people to settle the Oregon Territory, to populate this country with white people from coast to coast, although the size of the land claims added to the travel challenges in this land. This act did bring thousands of white settlers into the Oregon Territory—which included land now identified as Washington, Idaho, and parts of Wyoming—with nearly eight-thousand land patents issued by the mid-1800s. Every unmarried U.S. white man who applied was granted a designated 160 acres of land free of charge. A married couple was granted 320 acres, and for the first time in the nation, women could own their share. People with half American Indian blood were also able to own land—a nod to whites, in reality, as it encouraged white settlers to further expand their property by marrying Indian women and having children together. Back when they had applied, Chloe and William qualified for the full amount.

While my brothers and I grew up naively playing Cowboys and Indians, we had no real understanding of the relationships between whites and American Indians, although some of our friends had native blood. We were proud to imagine being of those first white Americans bold enough to identify the Eden of Oregon for what it was, and to stay here for all these generations. We did not learn the real stories related to our lands while studying our American history textbooks in Oregon public schools.

Many settlers didn't make it through the first four tough years of survival, and never got to own their land outright. After the land claim law expired, settlers could still claim land but had to buy it for just over a dollar an acre. Land got more expensive and claims grew smaller. All of the land claims were granted in Oregon City, even land plats outside of the Oregon Territory, such as San Francisco. Oregon City: the first town in Oregon. The End of the Trail; the head of the majestic Willamette Falls; the home of Dairy Queen and Wally's Music Shop and Dr. Campbell.

Chloe and William's early land claim was more controversial than most. The town of Salem developed like many early Western cities: settlers with knowledge and ability claimed the best land earliest. William claimed the land—that of today's capitol and Willamette University—in his name, but intentionally for what was then the Oregon Institute. He gave two-thirds of his land to the school.

After the Donation Land Claim Act of 1850 was passed, conflicts arose between the Willsons and the Oregon Institute Trustees over the title to the land. Under the 1850 law, the 320-acre property belonged jointly to William and Chloe Willson. Although William was bound to the trustees to administer the land for the Institute, Chloe was not, and she insisted that her legal right to the land be recognized. Throughout the disagreement, William remained a member of the board of trustees, and Chloe continued teaching. Before William's death, the dispute was resolved in compromise. A line was drawn to split the property in half along Salem's State Street: the 160 acres to the south would belong to the university, and the 160 to the north would belong to Chloe. Eventually, Chloe's land joined William's, and her house, originally located at Capitol and Court Street, was moved a short distance away onto the Willamette University campus as Lausanne Hall: home of the Women's College and the beginnings of Willamette's music school.

AS I STROLL across the campus of Salem's Willamette University today, I stop in front of Lausanne Hall. Rebuilt in 1920, it is the oldest residence hall on campus. How many who live there today know of the building's namesake, or of the woman whose home it used to be?

Leaving campus and walking north toward the capitol, I enter William's lasting gift to Salem: Willson Park, just south of their original house. While Google Maps still identifies Willson Park—with two *L*'s—signage quietly now reads *Capitol Park*. As Salem grew, William believed it should preserve open spaces similar to the common areas of early New England towns, which led to creation of the public square between the capitol and courthouse. As I wander the park, I stop to peer at the larger-than-life statues of John McLoughlin and Reverend Jason Lee. I walk past the flags of each of our Union States, slowing down to wander past the flags of our federally recognized American Indian nations. I remind myself of the tribes of the Willamette never officially recognized by our government. The Kalapuyan. Upper Chinookan. Molallas. And many more.

I sit on a bench next to Waite Fountain, close to Willson Park, and stare into a bustling Salem, especially busy during legislative sessions. I close my eyes, straining to venture back to a time of canoes and steamboats, carrying passengers to the riverbanks of Salem. Through my grief over Dad's death, I am stunned to realize that my own dad lived thirty-three years longer than my great-great-great-grandfather. William died before any of his children reached teenagehood. He died before he received the certificate of his land claim. Aged fifty-one. When Dad was fifty-one, he and I had no idea of where our healing relationship might go. What joys may lie ahead.

CHAPTER 16
BOOKS

J.K. GILL CAME TO Oregon because of Chloe. Joseph Kaye, better known as J.K., met Chloe and her daughters when he rented a room in the house they stayed in after William's death in Wilbraham, Massachusetts. J.K., then a twenty-year-old "Yorkshire-bred lad," was intrigued by Chloe's stories of a wild and unspoiled West. He had been experiencing severe eye problems and was advised by his doctor to give up his academic studies to rest his eyes, which made a trip West appealing to him.

J.K. reversed Chloe's eastbound journey: he traveled by steamer and rail over the Isthmus of Panama to San Francisco, hopped a boat to Sacramento, took a local train to Oroville, and spent the final six days on an overland stage to Salem—the journey took him thirty-two days in contrast to the nine months' duration of Chloe's original voyage.

The sea voyage and rest benefited J.K.'s eyes and allowed him to continue his studies and to teach several classes at the opening of fall term at Willamette University in Salem. He tried to return to his studies at Wilbraham in Connecticut the following year, but found that Greek and Latin still bothered his eyes. His doctor convinced him, instead, to complete coursework to become a teacher.

J.K. returned to Oregon soon after—lucky for us—marrying Chloe and William's daughter, my great-great-grandmother Frances "Fanny" Willson. J.K. brought us his English roots—and books. He wet his feet in book sales as he took over Chloe's half share of the Salem drugstore, giving most of his attention to the half of the store filled with books and stationery. A few years later, J.K. opened his own bookstore in Salem—a two-story brick building located at 356 State Street. Steamboats now traveled the Willamette between Portland and Salem, and stagecoaches stopped overnight in Salem, a town of just over 1,100, during their five-day route between Portland and San Francisco. But Portland was growing, and heading to be the largest center of Oregon, though I don't know exactly what precipitated their next decision.

In 1871, J.K. Gill and Frances, with Chloe joining them, moved north to where he built the legendary J.K. Gill Bookstore in downtown Portland.

Gill's Book Store, Salem, Oregon ca. 1866

WHILE MANY GENERATIONS of Portlanders still remember J.K. Gill's, most don't know today about its earliest publishing successes. An early book, first published as early as 1889 and followed by almost a dozen editions, was the *Dictionary of the Chinook Jargon.* This popular guide facilitated trade and trapping-related conversations between Chinook and English language speakers. The guide can be found digitally online, instructing us today that "Tilikum"—the name of Portland's newest bridge—means "person/family/people" when translated from Chinook language.

J.K. Gill's operated for one-hundred-and-fifty years with stores in four Western states at its peak, until the business was sold outside of family in 1970, and then, finally, the last of the stores closed in 1999, not able to compete against larger bookstores.

My great-grandfather William Montgomery, our Irish ancestor with the beautiful voice, graduated from Wesleyan University in Middletown, Connecticut, in 1890. He had decided he was not to be a Methodist Minister like his father, and instead came out West. William was smart, with a sense for business, and soon after arriving in Portland was recruited to help the J.K. Gill Company rise from the bankruptcy it had fallen into before the turn of the century. He went on to marry Georgia Gill, Frances and J.K.'s daughter, eventually becoming the president of Gill's.

J.K.—like many others at that time—believed the business world was for men. He selected the husbands of his daughters Frances and Kate to continue the Gill legacy: two husbands who in the end didn't agree on what was best for The Gill Company. I am thankful that the stories of that disagreement, and any related bad feelings, were not the stories our dad cared to share with us kids. I guess, in the end, we decide what stories to pass on to those we love.

J.K. Gill with daughters, Jessie, Georgia, Kate, Frances, Dorothy (1920s?)

J.K. lived ninety long years, outliving Frances and spending his final seventeen years without her, many of them in the home of his daughter, Georgia, in the Northwest Thurman House near the drinking fountain. This house, where his grandchildren, Daddy Dick and Nan, watched the lights streaming from the 1905 World's Fair.

Dad as baby with J.K. Gill, 1930

I hold his journal on my lap now, sipping a cup of English breakfast tea with a spot of milk. As I write these days, I often intermingle drinks of tea with IPA beer, depending on the time of day—and blast the music of the Irish Tenors. My great-great-grandfather kept this journal for most of his adult life. I read the entries—many of them about business at his store and the weather: snow storms, rainstorms, sunny days. Entries full of notable Portland names recognized today for the features left behind—streets, neighborhoods, a hospital, and a town: The Whitcombs, and the Doernbechers, Morelands, and Thielsens. J.K. wrote about trips to Multnomah Falls and Lincoln High recitals and railroad strikes. And funerals: Henry Pittock, James Failing. And he wrote about the end of the life of his love on a fall day in 1914.

"At 8:30 the nurse asked me to say 'Good-night,' which I did very briefly. Fanny looked longingly and I know she wanted me to stay longer. Had I known it was her last night on earth, I should have remained with her in spite of the nurse. I thank God for her companionship and love, for her beautiful life and example. How she loved her children and all of us!"

BOOKS WERE A constant presence for J.K. and his descendants. And Daddy Dick wasn't the only book author: J.K.'s daughter (another) Frances Gill penned a fictionalized book about Chloe in 1935, out of print decades ago. I remember now—not thinking it strange at the time—filling hours of kid-beach-time in the dunes of Ocean Park creating what I believed to be my printing press. Smoothing the dry sand; moistening it with the help of my plastic bucket full of salt water; lining up "utensils" comprised of various sizes of sticks, gull feathers, and seaweed. Readying it for "production." Inscribing my own writing onto the fresh surface. I didn't yet really know what a printing press might look like, I just knew it was something I needed to emulate. I recruited Dickie and Mike to join me, decades later sharing it with my own daughters, who probably didn't understand what joy I was trying to recreate. We wrote in our "press" and splashed in the crashing waves of the Pacific.

WHEN I WAS a kid, Sunday nights we would all watch *The Wonderful World of Disney*: Tinker Bell waved her wand, introducing us to the magic of the kingdom. We watched on our Magnavox television, near the floor-to-ceiling windows with river view, while Dad set up his shoe-shining kit, preparing his loafers for the week ahead. I loved the way his white cotton cloth moved back and forth, and the swishing sound it made as he shined up each black loafer. Dad was precise in his grooming.

But most evenings would find our parents in their individual chairs, Mom's never quite as fancy as Dad's. Reading while music amplified from the Magnavox turntable—slowly adapting with the technology of the times—in the background. This is how they spent the last evening of Dad's life, and it is the vision I have when I think of them together, an image duplicating my memory of my grandmother and grandfather.

Books lined the walls of both my parents' and grandparents' homes. As a fifth grader, I slowly made it through the books on the bookshelf in our living room on the Willamette—too young to understand some. I remember my ten-year-old criticism of *Catcher in the Rye*: "What's the big deal?"

I read whenever I could: in the back of the station wagon on family trips, or curled up on a couch when I was just plain tired of everyone around me. Reading was my escape, delivering me to faraway places. I could read through anything and in spite of everything, even brothers loudly imitating Portland Professional Wrestling: shirts stuffed with pillows, towels wrapped around necks as they pretended to be Lonnie Mayne, Tough Tony Borne, and Apache Bull Ramos. Creating new moves to fling each other—and sometimes their stuffed animals—across the floor or onto the couch. And I tried hard to carry my reading with me through mealtime so I could continue to be in my private world, but Dad created a rule—only pertaining to me. No books at the dining room and kitchen tables. I tried hard to hide them under the table, arguing loudly at what seemed to be a grave hypocrisy: newspapers accompanied breakfast, but no books.

Daddy Dick and Dad, *Cardinal Times* editors, 1948

Dad called himself a slow reader—always finding an opportunity to remind us he never was the A student our mother was, and in fact, that he was lucky to graduate from college. But he also reminded us how lucky he was to meet Mrs. Mabel Southwick, an English and journalism teacher at Lincoln High in the 1940s. After Dad knocked his teeth out playing football, WhoWho forbade him from playing any more football. Mrs. Southwick talked Dad into becoming a sports writer. Somehow, through the mysterious works of gifted teachers, and surely Dad's stubbornness, Dad overcame his dyslexia to be able to read and recite: the springboard he needed to become a royal podium ham. Dad's earliest published print piece was his column *Dick's Licks* in his high school paper, the *Cardinal Times*, for which he also served as editor for a time—just like his father, and later, a son. Dad continued to read, slow and steady, for the rest of his life. Unlike me, he retained everything he read. I should have learned from him early in life to slow down: as a fourth grader, I decided to take a speed-reading class, taking a bus from Wilsonville to West Linn High School during summer school to travel even faster through the books I devoured.

Late in life, Dad figured out how to use library websites to reserve books, moving from Multnomah County's library system to that of Clackamas County when he and Mom moved to their final home together. When he stopped driving, Mom and I made the weekly trip to West Linn Public Library: first picking up the books on hold, then—my favorite routine—trying to guess what additional books Dad might find interesting. Although a slow but voracious reader, he had fairly narrow literary interests. He somewhat embarrassedly admitted a love for "tell-all" books about famous people: Jack Lemmon and Michael Caine biographies led the pack. An occasional action novel might jump onto his reading table, and he had a few favorite novelists like Ivan Doig. But mostly—Dad loved history. As long as it was history unknown to him.

DAD DIDN'T PARTICULARLY like to travel to faraway places and had a phobia of flying. So it was quite the occasion when we got him to come with us to Italy for a family event. Many of us were spending a few days in Rome, after the big family affair. It was hot, something Dad never tolerated well—generally fitting, as he spent nearly his whole life in the Willamette Valley. I dropped in on my parents' Rome hotel, just to check in.

"Hi, Deeder," Dad said, sprawled on the double bed in his T-shirt and short pants. The mildly efficient air conditioner was pumped on high in this three-star hotel. He looked up from the tumble of books and tourist guides strewn on his lap and the bed.

"Whatcha doing, Dad? Where's Mom?"

"Oh, she's out exploring. You know your mom." He sighed. "It's damn hot out there!"

I looked at him. Raised my eyes in question, trying hard not to also roll them. Or nag him away from his comfortable, almost cool, resting place to the sites outside his window.

"The stories on the Colosseum are amazing! Did you know there were thirty-seven trap doors in the arena? It just blows my mind!" He held up one of several thick guidebooks. Dad knew far more about the city than I did, without moving an inch. He didn't feel the need to walk Rome's bowels—he was there just to be with us. As he would have said, "The history was icing."

WHAT I MISS, as much as anything else: Dad's reaction to the stack of books I would bring in each Saturday during his last leg of life. Though he expressed gratitude for each book title presented, I knew him well enough to decipher with each look whether he intended to actually crack the cover. Sometimes he'd try one that hadn't met his initial cut, surprising him. And he'd respond later, thrilled. "Thanks, Deeder . . . that one really grabbed me."

CHAPTER 17
INTERRUPTED

DAD WAS LUCKY in many things: real estate generally wasn't one of them. When we sold our Wilsonville riverfront home in 1973, he was grateful to find a buyer he liked—someone neither businessman nor investor. This owner has kept the home in their family ever since, the street still marked "Montgomery Way," though none of us live there anymore.

Dad jumped at the opportunity to accept an offer for his dream job: editor, king of the editorial page, of the daily *La Grande Observer* in Eastern Oregon. Perhaps surprisingly, given his love of the Columbia River, he turned down a sister job opportunity at the *Daily Astorian*. Dad wanted to know more about parts of Oregon undiscovered by him. And in a world of yesterday, when offered the job by Bob Chandler—owner of many of Oregon's small newspapers—Chandler alluded to Dad's drinking problem and let Dad know that he could only accept the job if he figured out a way to deal with it. The challenge for Dad was that the editor job was coupled with the job as publisher, duties that interested him far less.

Dad as PIO
Fort Lewis, ca. 1955

Our move to La Grande jarred our family away from life we knew and loved. It was the first—and only—time Dad lived outside of the Willamette Valley, other than his short army duty based at Washington State's Fort Lewis. He settled in at his new job while the rest of us finished the school year in Wilsonville. For this dream job, Dad did exchange Budweiser for root beer. I wonder now—did Dad think he was also giving up the Willamette forever?

During our time in Eastern Oregon, we entered a new chapter of rural living: our nearest neighbor now was almost a mile away, but a real town was accessible by a less than three-mile bike ride. A town with the Granada Theatre and a donut shop that sold powdered sugar cream puffs. And a Carnegie Library, its basement crammed full of books for young readers. I pounced on them, finding favorites in *Summer of my German Soldier* and *The Autobiography of Miss Jane Pittman*. No interest did I have in *Nancy Drew*. Books about hardship, strife, and injustice drew me into their pages. I rode my bike to the library several times a week that first summer, before school started, a plastic shopping bag from WhoWho slung over my handlebars.

La Grande. Surrounded by mountains of the Eastern Oregon kind: pouched pillows tufted with sage, gracefully puckering into seams of small canyons, creeks trickling through with winter snowmelt, dry in the summer. We explored the hills behind our house, crashing through bunchgrass and fescue, dry blades a dramatic departure from the effervescent mosses and lichens of the Pacific Northwest. And Dad was happy.

WE LEARNED ABOUT ticks, burrowing deep into our dogs' fur and my little brother's scalp. Reminding us that Dad did some things very well—and other things, not so much.

"Get it out," Rick, no longer Dickie, screamed. Panicking.

"Calm down, Rick," I yelled. "If its tail gets broken off, it'll never come out," I added more softly. Quoting something I thought I had heard somewhere. Making him whimper, struggling to hold back his tears.

"I've got it." Dad came in with a bottle of rubbing alcohol and a cotton ball, which he soaked and dabbed onto the ugly invader. We waited, but the little guy showed no intention of backing out of Rick's scalp.

"It's not coming out," I whispered. Rolling my eyes at the stupidity of not knowing how to do this. It was the height of tick season. Every time we walked up the mountain behind our Eastern Oregon house, dozens of them hopped on for a voyage, beginning the trek up our pant legs and under our socks. *I'd take carp and nutria any day*, I thought. Sadly.

"I've got it," repeated Dad. He lit a match, and touched the still-burning end to the tick. Rick's head went up in flames.

"What are you doing?" cried Rick. The fire was short-lived. Rick's hair was not fully singed, and as Dad held the burned, hot match tip to the tick, it slowly retreated.

"I think it's alcohol or a match. Not both," Pat said. Standing in the doorway. A smug look on his face.

I MET MY first whisper of a friend, the daughter of a *La Grande Observer* news writer, one day during that first hot Eastern Oregon August. A wildfire had broken out near our home. Our home: perched on the side of Rooster Peak, one of many mountains rimming the edge of town. Our home came with six acres and a barn. A long gravel driveway led up to the house—and at the bottom, a historical marker identified wagon wheel tracks of the Oregon Trail. Tracks from pioneers preparing to cross the truly blue Blue Mountains, with many of them arriving at the end of the trail near the Willamette Falls a few years after Chloe and William lived in Oregon City. Acres of peach and apricot orchards—fruits I had never seen growing in the Willamette Valley—sat between our house and the road.

La Grande welcomed us into her folds by introducing us to the fear of wildfire. Barely moved in, my brothers and I were sent to a neighboring family, the family of the news writer, sleeping little that night as we watched the flames move round our home from the valley below. Mom and Dad stayed back with a moving truck at bay, ready to reload if the wind changed directions, while they placed sprinklers on our roof. And Mom, preparing for a total loss, got the library books out of the house first—believing the borrowed books to be most important to protect, photo albums second.

Over fifteen-hundred people, including La Grande residents, worked to fight the Rooster Peak Fire. By morning, the wind had changed direction. Our home was spared, but many were not so lucky as the fire swallowed six-thousand acres, with the National Guard activated to help evacuate other homeowners. I think back to this now, as our Willamette Valley summers get hotter and drier, and fires rip through our Oregon forests. I wonder what will happen, here, to land we never before imagined to be so ripe for summer fire.

NUDGING INTO JUNIOR high, I was a shy new kid facing the intimidating task of navigating the road map to thirteen-year-old girl-friend-making. My end-of-summer whisper of a friend remained mostly that: she already boasted other strong friendships, and I peeked in as an awkward outsider. Boys, I knew, were an open book. Most of the ones I knew burped, farted, and told you what they thought. I hadn't figured out the secret life of girls. I had poured over Judy Blume's *Are You There, God? It's Me, Margaret* in desperate attempts to crack the code. I had reread many times the instruction manual offered in the free *Welcome to Womanhood* pink boxes freely offered by Kotex. Wondering if, in fact, this day would ever really come to me. Begging Mom to let me order a bra from the Sears catalogue, even though I didn't need one.

The school counselor, in an effort to help assimilate the apparent social misfits of junior high, included me in an invitation to a newly formed 4-H cooking club. Now, I had already complained loudly over the rule that all seventh grade girls were required to enroll in home economics for an elective, while boys filed into the shop class. Although I later had to admit it was useful to learn how to sew, and even better to pelt the kids in P.E. class on the track below the home economics kitchen windows with our heavy, flat biscuits that contained too much salt and not enough sugar. But a cooking class after school—that sounded more promising.

After school on the appointed day, I walked the five blocks to our meeting location, just a block away from Dad's office at the *La Grande Observer*, following directions in the invitation. I arrived at the house, eagerly imagining what new friends I might make. And I saw, as the door opened, that the host, my new girlfriend, was the girl mercilessly teased for her serious congenital facial deformity. The other four girls also must have met some unfair misfit qualifications, all of us sharing the trait of being mostly friendless.

I was kind to the girl and polite to her family. And I returned for each of the six weekly sessions. But the discomfort in the pit in my stomach even today reminds me of what I didn't do. I didn't stick up for her while the mean junior high boys yelled horrific names at her outside the school and in town. I long ago forgave my actions as a lonely, self-conscious preteen. But I am still sorry I moved away before I found the maturity to become a real friend. Sorry that I didn't ask Dad for advice. Sorry that I didn't understand, then, what a really kind man he was.

EASTERN OREGON INTRODUCED us to parched summers, and the smell of sage and wildfire. Swimming in La Grande's city pool, I escaped the heat and tried to make new friends. I learned late in life how to play Marco Polo: having to touch the pool bottom seemed a strange requirement after treading water in the seemingly bottomless Willamette. I signed up for the Summer Science Program, and spent hours each week in a hot school bus, traveling to the ghost town of Granite to pan for gold, to The Dalles Dam to learn about electricity and fish, and to high above the Grande Ronde Valley where I perfected the art of daydreaming, staring off into the patchwork land below.

As our first fall approached, we welcomed the chill that promised snow—the only thing I had been eager about in our move to Eastern Oregon. Mike, Rick, and I made a pact to sleep outside, under the cover of a patio, until it came. Every week we added another heavy blanket or sleeping bag to our cozy nest, reconfiguring, and each morning Mom came outside to wake us up for school. Snow finally came on Halloween.

Snow! We were mostly unaccustomed to snow and ice, and found ourselves walking to school in the bitter cold those mornings we couldn't get our car down the windy driveway. Dad donned a Norm Thompson sheepskin jacket to match the climate, and attempted to drive a Travelall through ice and snow, some days leaving before we kids were ready in the morning. I walked into my first-period junior high class frozen solid, eyelashes iced over, jacket and backpack dripping puddles as I thawed in the warmth of the classroom. My wire-frame glasses, new to me the year before, stuck to my face when I forgot to remove them before leaving home.

And to us, it was a new adventure! We sledded and had snowball fights and made snowmen. Our dogs harbored clumps of ice in their fur that pooled on our kitchen floor. We were tempted to lick something metal to see if it would really freeze onto our tongues. And Dad was so happy.

Teenage-hood slowly seeped into my spirit. That first Halloween I watched as kids squirted shaving cream on cars instead of trick-or-treating. I learned that sports gave me a way to be noticed—the saving grace for lonely kids with good coordination. We had sold our *DeDe 2* to pay for a season of skiing at Anthony Lakes, home of the driest snow in Oregon, and Saturdays found us on early morning winter drives to our lessons.

I still tried to find ways to argue with Dad—teenage life now knocking on my door, as I insisted that he roll the car windows down as he puffed on his pipe. But Dad was busy and involved: filled by a community that was kind to him, and wasn't shy to share their appreciation. We moved through another summer, me now with a few new friends who offered invitations to sleepovers and overnight church camps. But too soon, as we all began to settle in, the floor dropped out. Again.

I turned down my first and only junior high date just before we left La Grande. My almost-first-date played the trombone in band with me and was a year older. My new, but not yet fully trusted girlfriend advised me that my admirer liked to make out behind the bleachers during football games, and he had suggested we meet there. Oh, and sometimes he drank. Beer. Now, *that* made me question things. Sure, he could play the trombone and was kind of cute, but beer frightened me. And really, what kind of relationship could be built on only knowing that he was a good trombone player? Daddy Dick might have said it depended on what his favorite selection of music was. I cancelled, sending the comment, *just what do you think I am?*

I was becoming a rule follower: later I learned that lots of kids of alcoholics were. Or maybe it was because I fell in the middle of four rowdy brothers. Or maybe, it was just because.

AS I READ Dad's *La Grande Observer* editorials now, forty years later, I smile. He put words together in a fashion that rarely grace op-ed pages today. Some days he would hit home on controversial issues with a headline like: "End of Tussock—for Now." Dad originally sided with those who claimed that DDT—banned already by EPA's William Ruckelshaus in 1972—was the only solution to protect Oregon's timber from the infesting tussock moth, a native insect of our Blue Mountains. The tussock moth defoliated the needles from our Grand and Douglas fir, from the top down.

Later, Dad acknowledged the warnings issued from environmental scientists that had been largely ignored by decision-makers, as he wrote in his editorial, "An almost final chapter about the deal where nobody wins after 426,559 acres treated with DDT in Oregon, Washington and Idaho." Some claimed timber was saved, but eighteen-thousand cattle and sheep were no longer fit for market due to insecticide levels. Little did I realize then that it was, in part, the August 1973 fire that threatened our home and others, that encouraged our Senator Bob Packwood to petition then-president Gerald Ford and the EPA to allow to spray the then-banned DDT. And thanks to lobbying interests and against the recommendation of scientists, DDT was allowed in the Blue Mountains, along with acreage in Umatilla and Wallowa-Whitman Forests. Spraying that left us with contamination and effectively did nothing to protect our timber or natural resources.

Dad, *LaGrande Observer*, ca. 1973

Dad's editorials often strutted prideful community exclamations. I remember one in particular: "Cowboys they are not." This editorial honored the Sagebrush and Jackrabbit Kids after Podunk La Grande High beat Powerhouse Corvallis for the 1974 state football championship, coached by La Grande's beloved teacher and coach, Doc Savage. La Grande had won the semifinal game at home, snowplows prepping the field minutes before kickoff: Benson High was left to brave Interstate 84's Dead Man's Pass and Cabbage Hill on the dejected journey back to Portland. And then, during the road trip championship at Portland's Civic Stadium, our own Andy— apparently not hampered by that BB's shot to his peripheral vision after all—completed three long pass completions as a standout wide receiver. The first time a high school team from Eastern or Northeastern Oregon had ever, in thirty-two times out, won an AAA Oregon high school football championship.

But my personal favorite of Dad's headlines was "Calm down, Tom," in response to the news that McCall was considering a third party presidential bid. Dad began the editorial: "Tom McCall was not born in a log cabin." And finished: "Tom McCall will make a great governor. That was his slogan. He has lived up to it. But please, let's leave well enough alone."

Dad was a beloved community leader, awarded the prized La Grande Communicator of the Year award just shortly after he was let go. But he was a talented writer without interest or aptitude in publishing and business plans, and it was the beginning of newspaper wars—the death of a certain type of community newspaper and certain kinds of editors, with a new reality of what it took to sell, publish, and prosper. And Dad hated, more than anything, to fire staff. Dad's replacement—who became a good friend of Dad's, even visiting our *Illahee* House for many years—was warned by Bob Chandler that he would need to choose between running a good newspaper or being the most popular guy in town. Bob knew what choice Dad had made.

The moves were tough, and the next few years difficult on all of us. But when all was said and done, Dad gifted us a full year and a half of exploration in Eastern Oregon. And Dad, several years' post-retirement, explained in yet another Letter from Dad, that his position in La Grande was the finishing school he needed to do his best work. That, "he was most grateful to have been hired and fired at and from the *Observer*. No hard feelings."

CHAPTER 18

MY TITAN

WHEN I FIRST saw the Grande Ronde River, I thought it was a creek. It was beautiful, and I came to love it: waters emptying into the John Day River; eventually—like the Willamette—toppling into the Columbia. But it wasn't what I expected for a river, different than the mighty Columbia and the winding Willamette. We all came to love Eastern Oregon—the Wallowa Mountains, Baker, Fossil, and Granite—in the short time we were there. My memory of these places steered me toward my college town in the Missoula Valley, where the Clark Fork River flows and leads, eventually, to the Columbia. But although I loved the Ponderosa pine and sage in the years away from the Willamette Valley, I missed moss-covered logs and old man's beard drooping from the limbs of Douglas firs. I missed the musky smell of skunk cabbage, beginning to ferment in a warm spring sun, poking out from murky ponds. And I missed our river.

HAVING RAISED CHILDREN, having lain awake at night fretting over finances, I only now understand the financial fears Dad had after the loss of his La Grande job. Fears I didn't acknowledge before, and in fact blamed him for fully. And now, in remembering our past, I understand privilege. When Dad lost this job, we moved back to Portland—just after Christmas—into my grandparents' home. Coming full circle: less than a mile from Good Samaritan Hospital, where my brothers and I were born; where, in just a few short years, WhoWho would close her eyes for the final time; and where, in another three decades I would pray for Dad as he underwent surgery to ameliorate a staph infection lodged into his heart. Barely a mile from Dad's beginnings near Balch Creek; and from the final Portland years of so many relatives, like Chloe, who died at the age of fifty-six in 1874 while living with her daughter and son-in-law, Frances and J.K., in their house in Northwest Portland. To be followed by J.K. and

Frances and Sam and William A. and Pop-Ard and Muna and Daddy Dick and Aunt Nan and Bill. And others.

Privileged, yes. But I hated moving into a city with our house adjacent to Portland's noisy Canyon Road. I missed the peace and quiet of country living: all I had ever known. I missed my childhood, realizing too late that it was over. I couldn't get used to the sounds of the city that never seemed to stop. I spent evenings in my closet reading books, door closed, earplugs blocking out the constant roar of cars and, later in the night, Dad's snoring.

I didn't understand then how much Dad, too, hated it. Upon our move, Dad suffered through two years in advertising working for McCann-Erickson, portrayed as the aggressive swallower in the *Madmen* TV show. Dad was never a happy advertising executive, and though Portland was no Madison Avenue, discontented memories kept him uninterested in ever watching this TV series that was popular late in his life. But he worked in an industry he hated, to support us on such short notice. He retreated into the darkness of old habits that made his marriage unsalvageable and created a divide between us that I couldn't imagine ever crossing.

I was not empathetic. I attacked him silently and withdrew from him, creating the worst two years of our relationship.

EARLY IN OUR adjustment to Portland, Dad had the brainiac idea that we three younger kids, the ones not yet fully engaged in teenage life, should explore Oregon's extraordinary places. Our old friends on the Willamette had a monster Winnebago, the kind we now criticize as gas-guzzlers. But back then, to Rick, Mike, and me, it seemed as glorious and amazing as a trip to far-off Europe. And a bonus: I could take as many books as I liked.

So we set out. We sat overlooking Crater Lake, silently admiring deep blue. Wishing we could swim out to Wizard Island, not imagining the numbing cold that would freeze our limbs before moving twenty yards. During that visit I would never have pictured myself, only a handful of years later, working for a summer at the lake. We continued on to the Oregon Caves, the John Day Fossil Beds, and the Steens Mountains, where our radiator overheated. Highway 101 along the winding, seasonally wild Oregon coast. I had a road map of Oregon, and took great pleasure in highlighting our route with a thick marker. Dad was right. We did see the beautiful country of Central, Southern, and Coastal Oregon, adding to our recently acquired Eastern Oregon repertoire of Baker—not yet Baker City—and Enterprise, Wallowa Lake, Spout Springs, and Sumpter. We explored new rivers: the Deschutes and the Rogue.

Crater Lake, 1975

But mostly, to me—a teenager struggling to understand my parents' conflicts—it was awful. Dad's thunderous snoring disrupted the initial thrill of sleeping inside the Winnebago: so loud that we three kids had to set up a sleeping spot hundreds of feet away from the luxury cruiser. I read my books, occasionally looked out the window, swam in new lakes, and mostly moped.

Conflict between Dad and me rose to a peak toward the end of our two-week trip, as he maneuvered the RV over a coastal bridge just south of Tillamook. It was a narrow, one-lane bridge and we were in a very big vehicle: crossing the bridge unscathed was barely possible, even without opposing traffic. With an oncoming car approaching—and full stereo of me screaming—Dad perfectly shaved off the passenger side-view mirror as it struck the wall of the bridge. And Dad—who we all knew then—could be so reactive. He yelled, honestly afraid of hurting us and damaging our borrowed vehicle. He raised his voice as he told us all to be quiet so he could drive.

I freaked out: "Dad, you are going to get us killed!"

When we got home, Mom was first out of the RV saying, "I'm not mad. Just don't anyone talk to me for twenty-four hours."

And I began to withdraw even further from Dad. I decided he was reactive and chauvinistic and, most mistakenly in the midst of teenage-hood, that he didn't love me. And worse, I couldn't imagine why I would ever want a relationship with him again.

WE WERE USED to a different type of vacation. In addition to time at the beach, Mom introduced us—well, the kids—to backpacking early on. We intimately explored mountain ranges throughout the original Oregon Territory.

Mom was rich with five sisters, which always seemed so unfair to me. I prayed for a sister. Once, I thought I had one coming when brother Pat asked for a tran-"sistor" radio one Christmas. I had heard him ask Santa and though I did know where babies came from, I imagined hopefully that perhaps there was in fact another source. After all the Christmas presents were opened, wrap cleaned up, I began asking.

"Where's my sister? Pat told Santa to bring a sister," I demanded. Finally, I came to understand that there was in fact no hope in our family for another girl to help me hold down the fort.

Mom was lucky that several of her sisters had married men who liked to backpack—men who, ultimately, helped spur on my youngest brothers on our large family trips. My favorite part of backpacking, besides eating the M&M's out of the GORP bag, was following creeks that crisscrossed our hiking trails. Creeks popping out of underground springs, as if from nowhere, edges bordered with phlox and columbine. Bubbling over rocks, above which marmots whistled their greeting. Swimming in the ice-cold, glacier-fed lakes.

Backpacking wasn't something our parents shared. Dad loved to hike—but he drew the line at carrying stuff on his back. He claimed it reminded him of the army. Later, we all learned how Dad had barely made it out of infantry training when they found him much better suited to write for the army, and moved him into their public information office. He really never carried many loads on his back. Later in life, he was willing to join us as we poked fun at his excuse. And once, I broke him down. Almost.

A FISTFUL OF years later, my second summer at Crater Lake, I found myself sweating in a windowless basement six days per week, washing, drying, and folding linens for tourists who complained about a bad meal or no turn-down service: sometimes seemingly unappreciative of the wildness beyond the window. When I had applied for the job, I assumed my two years of experience during high school serving oyster stew at Portland's Dan and Louis Oyster Bar, and collecting quarter tips after pouring never-ending cups of coffee at the Kopper Kitchen next to Portland State University, would place me in Crater Lake's dining room. But instead I struggled to learn to fold fitted sheets into perfect packages and prayed for days when housekeeper shortages would pull me up out of our mostly windowless dungeon to put those sheets on beds and empty trash cans in rooms with full view of deep blue. Nights, I would jam in my earplugs, sweltering in a dormitory dripping with barely twentysomething girls. Only on Sundays could I escape, struggling to uncover solitude, hiking alone along the rim as far as I could and still make it back for my dinner of yet another PB&J, no meat-eating for me in those days.

The phone call I made to tell Dad I was quitting was the first spark of the beginning of our new relationship.

"I'm not leaving for him," I told Dad, referring to a boyfriend who missed me, knowing—though I hadn't yet admitted it—that Dad honored the independence I had claimed for myself. "I'm unhappy, sick, and more than anything, I feel like they are taking advantage of us."

And Dad, he who understood being unhappy at work, agreed. "I'm so glad that you called me to ask my advice."

And though we were about to enter unknown family territory, he and Mom divorcing later that year, for Dad and me it was the earliest thawing of a breakthrough.

THE NEXT YEAR, at nineteen, I had my best summer job ever while working at Mt. Rainer National Park. The Student Conservation Association hires college students to work in beautiful parks around the country as part of the team caring for our national treasures. My job was to help maintain trails, be available in the backcountry for visitors, and watch for smoke from a fire tower late in the summer during fire season. The SCA added ranks to rangers by providing housing but paying meagerly. I didn't care. It was enough to help pay for my next year of college, and allowed me to hike. Hike, write, and read. I discovered new rivers and creeks, and a love for a new mountain. I discovered people who cared about wild land as much as I did. My duty station, Three Lakes, was smack on the Pacific Crest Trail, nearest Mt. Rainer's Ohanapecosh Ranger Station. I was assigned a cabin with woodstove, bed, sink, and an outdoor well. And a family of mice that drove me to sleep outside on a picnic table rather than listen to their nighttime scurries. I learned after the fact the cost of leaving leftover dishwater overnight in my undrained sink, tossing out the poor lifeless mouse in the morning.

Dede, Shriner Peak, Mt. Rainer National Park, 1981

My only avenue of communication—handheld radios were reserved for real rangers—was a large, awkward radio I had to haul half a mile up a hillside to get reception. And yet, I was never afraid. I would hike miles on sections of the Pacific Crest Trail bordering the park, turning magnificent corners to the startling sheer grandeur of Mount Rainier. At other corners, I peeked into nearby Mount St. Helens' newly formed crater, my eyes following wisps of steam and trails of gritty ash that still escaped. I spent my first July Fourth alone, climbing high above my cabin to watch sunset fireworks.

I filled my stomach with wild huckleberries and the solitude I craved, while learning that I actually did like people, and even started to miss them when none were around. I read Edward Abbey's *Desert Solitaire* and May Sarton's *Journal of a Solitude* and René Dubos's *So Human an Animal,* and Norman McLean's *A River Runs Through It* as

I drank my morning cup of instant coffee with powdered milk, and by flashlight at night. And slowly, so very slowly, I began the process of mending my relationship with Dad. I forgave him for the divorce I had fully blamed him for: the divorce that had come earlier that year, freeing Mom to explore adventures she had missed early on.

One weekend, while back at my Ohanapecosh Ranger Station apartment, Dad called.

"I'd like to come up and visit you next week, Deeder."

He would visit on a day I was scheduled at Three Lakes: I started to get nervous in anticipation. Dad and I hadn't spent much time alone in the past seven or eight years. I envisioned the possibilities of tough one-on-one full-court press with just us two together. Alone. On the appointed afternoon, I loitered near my cabin as I awaited Dad's visit into my solitude, hoping his sense of direction would lead him to my camp. Finally, Dad appeared in the distance, walking down the dusty trail as it dropped into the basin of my private hideout. He had hiked six and a half miles, with a sleeping bag under his arm and a small daypack on his back.

"Wouldn't it have been easier with a backpack?" I called out to him in greeting.

He got closer. "I don't backpack. You should know that." And he gave a hint of a sweaty smile.

We feasted on Ragu-covered spaghetti, cooked on my woodstove. Biting off tiny safe morsels of conversation. I, for my part, didn't share about my supervisor—a man my father's age—who suggested back rubs and midnight visits. I didn't share with Dad about my anger at the way something so offensive and personal could be swept up and neatly hidden on a back shelf when I reported it. Dad played his part too: so much I didn't want to hear about. Yet. I told him, instead, about my three-and-a-half-mile hike up switchbacks of hell to Shriner Peak Fire Tower, overloaded with drinking water that nearly burst my pack. I had squinted hard to keep exhausted tears from flowing, and refused to hurt more than the other guy—the other SCA hire that summer. I developed mental toughness over three miles, finishing in an endorphin-shouting euphoria. Dad laughed.

I told him about the hot, late afternoon during my two-week-straight duty at Shriner Peak when I jogged down topless, free of public and visitors—granted leave from the Osborne fire finder for minutes during this height of fire season—to grab a quick dip in the water of a secret, cool lake. I almost ran straight into Mama Bear from *Blueberries for Sal* as she rested back on hind paws, throwing huckleberries into her mouth. She sat in the afternoon sun, surrounded by Pacific Northwest berry bushes, near the snow-covered peak of Mount Rainer. I told Dad I skipped my swim that day, and he nodded. And he laughed, again.

I shared little bits with Dad. Our same sense of humor began to pave a new route ahead, and our dramatic differences, for the first time, became okay. Dad called my pad a "five-star." The next morning, we took a dip in the lake, shallow and warmed by the midsummer sun: our mutual love of water. A full day we'd spent together, just due east of the Nisqually Mission where our Chloe and William joined forces. And then, with a hug and kiss—always that, even in our silent years—I watched Dad, hair slicked back and sleeping bag tucked under his arm, slug back up the trail, away from the Three Lakes basin.

THE MOVE BACK to Portland six years before this magical Mt. Rainer summer was hard, but the silver lining immense. Dad suffered through those two years in advertising: he didn't like selling things that sometimes made him feel he was playing games with clients he didn't always respect. Until the stars aligned. In his midlife, Dad became public information manager at the Port of Portland and then, soon after, maritime public affairs manager. To hone his river knowledge, strengthening his love affair with the waterways that held his heart. And to write, and be happy in his work, happy to always share that really, "he was just a technical guy." A writer with no big dreams of moving high into management or beyond.

Dad wrote about trade with Japan and China, and the Swan Island Shipyard expansion, and Mount St. Helens' ash when it interrupted Portland's river highway. He spoke on the podium and to news cameras. He gathered stories about the Willamette and Columbia—our rivers. And became the man I remember best, loved most. Though he wasn't without controversy, even in our family. Dad supported dredging to increase Portland's international trade, though he accepted the concerns of the environmental community. And though pro-union, Dad had a hard time understanding labor disputes that disrupted work—he worried Portland's shipping industry would taper away. Old fashioned in some ways, stubborn and impatient for sure—but motivated, always, by his love for what he worried was becoming a dying river-industry. An industry he loved more than any other.

Dad had come full circle: from a boyhood of steamship stories and river-loving adventures, to his earliest ad agency account as a young man with the Dock Commission while working in the family advertising agency, to his dream career with the Commission's predecessor, the Port of Portland. And as he did with almost everything, he shared a favorite quip. "I wanted to be a communicator and a storyteller, and the port gave me that opportunity. It was nice to get into the candy store."

Dad on the Willamette River

As an ultimate gift, shortly before retirement, Dad received Portland Shipping Club's Old Salt award for outstanding service to the Columbia River maritime industry: a titan of our rivers. Post-retirement, as a maritime consultant, he authored a weekly column for the *Daily Shipping News* about all things maritime. And Dad was the Port of Portland's most loyal proponent right up until his last days, submitting letters to the *Oregonian* editor and to others he felt who needed help understanding the importance of our river highways.

Dad among memorabilia

OF ALL GOOD things Dad did in his life, becoming alcohol-free was the one of the biggest gifts he gave to himself, and everyone to whom he spoke or wrote, everyone he mentored and loved. He wasn't private about his losses. If he could help one more person in recovery, he would. And that he did through calls, visits, and letters to others new to the journey. He told his story so many times at AA meetings, that late in life upon being reminded how many times others had heard his story, he realized he no longer needed this weekly community sharing. It is only now, after Dad's passing, that I seem to be able to fully realize the depth of his struggle: its toll on his relationships, and the acceptance and profound gratefulness he found through his recovery. Dad's belief in the *Big Book* and its Twelve Steps permeated his existence. Not until after his passing did I learn of Dad's favorite passage: "The greatest sin in the world is standing in the way of another's growth. The second is standing in the way of your own growth."

It is profound that Mom and Dad found each other again after eight years apart. She got to do things that many young women of the 1950s missed. And as difficult as it was for us kids to watch our parents' divorce in our late teens and early twenties, it was unforgettable to celebrate their second and final wedding ceremony in Washington Park's Rose Garden, and later, their golden anniversary—wisely ignoring those gap years. Mom and Dad shared their senior years—travel, grandchildren, simple joys, unlike so many whose lives and relationships are cut short. And they were together when the time came for Dad to go, leaving behind the deep sadness of losing one's life partner; one's true love.

Rick, Mom, Dad, Dede and Andrew, 1988

Upon our move to Portland from La Grande in 1974, I was thrown into an upper-crust society that some of our extended family had helped create. Charter members, a few of them: the University Club, Multnomah Athletic Club. We moved into the part of Portland that Mom's father—when Mom and Dad first courted—worried would never be fair or kind to a woman who came from what some considered then, in the 1950s, to be "the wrong side of the Willamette."

As for me during those high school years when I was much of the time silent with Dad, I made friends. I mostly enjoyed high school. I was lucky. Rescued again by sports and, now, the passing of Title IX in 1972: a law that gave us girls, referred to before by some as "tomboys" or "dykes" the right to play sports, with a deadline set during my junior year that all U.S. high schools and colleges were required to meet. Women ten years older than I were thrilled, yet also dismayed to have missed out on such opportunities. We high-school-aged girls now were able to try out and play on freshman, JV, and varsity teams and even advance to citywide and state tourneys if our teams were successful enough. And the larger schools with resources, and girls with time, began to be known as Oregon athletic powerhouses.

Dad came to almost every game or meet I was in—even though I was barely speaking to him. Even toward the end of my high school career when he had stopped drinking, I just couldn't forgive. And I learned at sixteen: taking away alcohol doesn't suddenly heal all the damage done. I can still hear his loud, excited voice echoing from the bleachers at Lincoln High, and even during some college games: "Go, Gumdrop!" That cheer: it used to embarrass me; I didn't acknowledge his praise in those years. Now, I long to hear it one more time.

Mom, Dede, Dad and Andrew, state basketball playoffs 1976

I never felt as though I fully belonged during this time in Portland. I wonder now if this feeling was similar to what our Wilsonville friends might have felt about those of us living in nice homes on the riverbank; what they felt when Mom, new to Wilsonville, threw a tea party with fancy china and linens—wedding gifts rarely used, though they couldn't have known that. In high school in Southwest Portland, I learned that, no, we weren't rich. Though money wasn't the reason why, I realized how different I felt than my classmates. Is that how most of us feel in those adolescent years? Different? But we were. Our childhood had been saturated with muddy water, crawdads, and birch trees. And alone time, to become friends with our siblings and ourselves: what Mom and Dad wanted for us after all. Today, after losing Dad, our sibling bonds—cemented by shared years, shared memories, shared sadness—are strong enough to share the afterward together. Stories. We share stories. Memories feed our hearts and souls. They hurt and cause us to question. They teach our children, and inspire us to understand and do better. Our stories heal, accompanying us each day and into the future. Like so many families who are lucky enough to remember their stories.

Michael, Dede, Rick, Dad, Mom, Patrick, Andrew, 1999

My own daughters, of the twentysomething generation, share our love of the rivers and the stories of family—our strengths and weaknesses. Love for our beautiful Oregon. They, too, have spent days—years—exploring the wonders of our region. But they are also now our harshest critics. They listen to our stories with an ear to the future: they worry as to what has been left for coming generations. How mistreated so many were and still are. They feel robbed of freedom and vision; of opportunities to make decisions that most impact them and the living community they love. I understand. And it makes me sad. And it would have made Dad sad.

CHAPTER 19
WATCHING THE RIVER RUN

AS HE GOT older, as much as Dad hated the thought of losing the independence of driving, he couldn't imagine hurting someone in an accident. Shaken up after a medical incident, Dad put away his own keys, but toyed with the idea of driving again after assurance from his doctor. And he asked my opinion.

"Well, Dad," I started. "To be honest, you were a pretty crappy driver even when you were young."

Dad looked at me, raised his thick, white eyebrows, and chuckled.

"But I'd be happy to take you on a driving test."

Again, he looked at me. Clearly tempted to make a crack about knowing how to drive before I was a twinkle in his eye, or some overdone phrase. But he held back. "Okay," he said seriously. "It's a deal."

So Dad and I went driving. I reminded him, "Keep both hands on the wheel." Again, he raised his eyebrows, but made no comment.

We drove on the freeway and I reminded him to keep his speed constant. "You keep speeding up and slowing down," I said. He tried to offer a smile, a little frustrated.

We got held up awaiting a left turn arrow on the blink; Dad didn't turn through three traffic cycles. He started to sweat, and looked at me. Knowing if he just took a run for it, I would flunk him. I felt like a driving instructor for teenagers as I advised him. "Just go straight and look for a safe place to turn left, and double back."

When he pulled the car back into his parking spot, I said, "So do you want my report?"

He tried to be patient. He gave me that look—the questioning look. *Really? Must I?* "Okay, sock it to me," he said.

"Okay, Dad," I said. "Keep both hands on the wheel—that means no fiddling with the radio. And no snacking!" He kept a supply of black licorice in his glove compartment. He looked over at the glove compartment, back at me, and sadly nodded in agreement.

"And maybe you should avoid the freeway," I added.

Dad agreed to obey the rules. "You are quite bossy, you know."

And from then on, even after Dad stopped driving for good and I drove him to his appointments and errands, he'd point out a decision I made behind the wheel and offer, "I'd flunk you for that." And he'd smile.

When he did stop driving, I doted on him. I had already begun managing his medications, but now we did his trips and errands together. Ten years prior—as I temporarily chauffeured Dad while he recovered from ankle surgery—his joints worn out from years of hiking and pounding handball courts, I had made an amazing observation. I was a lot like Dad. I was astounded. Similar to this Dad who in my teens had been so reactive and judgmental.

How could this be? I had wondered then.

But in this final of Dad's life chapters I realized—our similarities were even greater than I had imagined. How is it that we all become a bit more like our parents than we ever imagined? Of all the traits we shared, more than anything, we shared humor. We teased each other as we made up for a lost decade. Our joking and laughing sustained us, mile after mile, and challenge after challenge. Dad repeated those old stories with a laugh—about me being so good onstage at handing out lunches to middle-school-aged "dwarves" and about playing with the hardball. As he helped craft a title for a blog I was writing, he wrinkled his nose distastefully and asked who in the world would refer to writing as a "blog," adding that it sounded like something that got stuck on the bottom of your shoe.

We joked about the terrible years of my teenage-hood when he tried so hard, but I wouldn't forgive. Dad seemed to remember me giving him an unsolicited hug after I learned he had gotten a vasectomy—something I had no memory of. I reminded him about the matching gifts he bought Mom and me one Christmas.

He smiled. "How could you not have loved that?"

Dad was not a birthday or Christmas kind of guy—except for the food and family—and generally relied on Mom to make these celebrations special; something she did with amazing flair. When I was fifteen, something got into Dad and he went into Meier & Frank at the height of holiday season, thinking he would select something special for the two gals he loved so much.

Christmas Morning, 1976, Dad pulled two identical store-wrapped gifts out from under the tree. He put one in front of Mom and handed the other to me with an unusual look of anticipation. This wasn't usually the happiest time for Dad—with long-ago memories of awakening from late Christmas Eves to morning boisterousness. Mom opened hers first, thrilled at the effort Dad was making to be part of our present frenzy. As she pulled the white tissue paper away, she proudly held up a kelly green corduroy one-piece pantsuit—complete with long bell-bottom legs, bell sleeves, a full zipper up the front, and a narrow fabric belt.

Now it was my turn. I began to open the package. I swallowed as I lifted aside the same white tissue paper. And there it was: an identical, slightly smaller, pantsuit. Kelly green. I swallowed again, smiled briefly at Dad and mumbled a thank-you. I locked my eyes on Mom's and tried hard not to roll them.

THESE MANY YEARS after that Christmas of the kelly green jumpsuits, slowly, Dad's body began to slow down, even though he faithfully rode the exercise bike even the day before his heart beat that last time. His physical body was fading. And although I know he didn't want to die, he also didn't go kicking and screaming. He was, above all else, so very grateful for all he had. And every day, I was thankful for the additional time we had to laugh together, and for me to love my Dad. Dad's mind—it was strong to the end. I offered books. And he shared his stories. Today it is his humor I miss as much as the stories—and hope to always smile at memories that leap from the crevices of my mind.

DEEP DOWN, I always knew he was proud of me. That he loved me. And he knew I loved him. But I never told him I was sorry—for taking so long, for wasting time. After he died, I needed to tell him. And I couldn't. But now, I realize, he didn't need to hear those words.

Now, as I write, I feel as if Dad is still alive. He crafts stories in my brain. And edits them. Reminding me of a detail I had forgotten. He helps me add that twist of humor: an emblem of him. And I feel happy as I feel him. Sometimes when I stop writing, I remember, again, like it just happened. Remember that he has died. That he no longer is here on earth.

I hang out near the Willamette. I stroll along the banks. I smell the smells. I listen to the music: the rhythm of the waves lapping against the shore. I feel the river with my eyes closed. I am reminded of Dad, and of our history. Good and bad. Our land and its future. Good and bad.

For me, now, Dad is in this winding emerald river, as it curves past farmland and beyond carp sucking at the sides of docks; as it flows past the Canby Ferry and the raging Willamette Falls, filtering through the millrace where soon, we hope, the locks will operate again; as it flows under fishing boats and dragon boats and the steamer *Portland*, bubbling under the bridges from Sellwood to St. John's; as it pulls in the waters from Forest Park's Balch Creek, mixing with a few of Dad's ashes sifting through sediments; as it flows beyond Portland's dry docks and joins the mighty Columbia, floating miles and years past steamships and canoes, bubbling under the Astoria-Meagler Bridge, joining, finally, the vast Pacific Ocean.

Dad in the DeDe on the Willamette River near Wilsonville

The Writing of this Book

TWO MONTHS AFTER Dad's death and just a few weeks after his memorial service on the steamer *Portland*, Russ and I caught an airplane for a long-before planned trip to Ireland. It had been so hard for me to get excited for this trip after Dad died—even though visiting Ireland had been on my bucket list for a long time. A week before leaving I baked chocolate chip cookies for our good friend Kelly to thank him for filming Dad's service. I felt so much responsibility to stick around for Mom in Dad's absence.

As I mixed eggs and assorted ingredients, I kept asking myself how I could possibly leave on vacation. Suddenly—alone in the kitchen—I began crying. I felt Dad say to me, "Deeder, your mother will be fine. You have done so much. You need to go." I laughed and cried—of course! I hadn't been able to figure out why I hadn't yet dreamed about Dad, but certainly, I should have known! Chocolate chip cookies would bring Dad back to me! (We always teased Dad that he was a lot like our dog, Oscar, when food was involved.) I felt comforted that the trip would work out okay.

On the plane I began writing. I started with the notes I had shared during the memorial service, and continued to add in everything I could remember about my years with Dad. I didn't want to forget anything. And soon in Ireland, in the small town of Dingle near crashing, rocky coastlines, I felt Dad.

Shortly after my return from the Emerald Island, I looked for a story I remembered writing decades ago in college. I climbed up on a chair in the corner of my bedroom closet and lifted it down from the dusty shelf: a box full of pictures, newspaper clippings, and a graduation program. I dug through this box as I sought the typewritten, stapled story I so clearly remembered writing: a story about the Willamette River—its dank smells and woods being demolished by bulldozers, but full of fictional characters. I had attempted a brief foray into creative writing, signing up for Introduction to Creative Writing taught by Bill Kittredge during my first freshman quarter at the University of

Montana. The class was small with hopeful, aspiring writers. And, perhaps, like so many other college students, while I had big hopes of being an early smashing, successful writer, I wrote a pretty bad first story that earned a C-. I was devastated not to have it selected as one of the sample stories Dr. Kittredge shared with our class. I hadn't even recognized yet what a well-known, published writer our professor was, nor that he also grew up in Oregon. I instead noticed that he'd sit on the corner of a desk, light up his cigarette, and occasionally pause as he tapped it on the desk corner, releasing ashes that would drift to the classroom floor, and that our class was often cancelled.

None of that really mattered as I slowly, through the quarter, learned that real writing required so much work! Rewriting, details, reworking. I retyped my story, improving it and others as the quarter progressed. But I just didn't feel like I had anything really significant to write about. My biology classes, instead, pulled at me deeply. And though I kept filling journals, hiding them in the bottom drawers of my desk, I walked away from creative writing.

But these many years later in 2014, after Dad's death, I just couldn't stop writing. I wrote all the time—compelled, almost crazed, to get my story out. I wrote early mornings and late nights, and I did in fact play over and over all the Irish Tenor music that I owned, or that I could find on Pandora. I pored over the volumes of family history and photographs my mom had so painstakingly put together decades before. I wrote in short bouts on TriMet during my commute, in coffee shops, on airplanes, and late at night in hotels during work trips. I learned, as sometimes shared by other writers, that I didn't know where my story would take me, and I certainly didn't know how it would end. I joined Willamette Writers and attended their 2015 July conference with my dear friend Maura. I learned more about plot and voice. And I kept writing. But I pushed back from joining any writing groups, realizing that I am a solo writer.

I brought in my daughter, Erin, a graduate of the University of Montana, to be my writing mentor and editor. As Erin offered constructive criticism and edited my chapters, I went back in and rewrote upcoming chapters prior to her review. She taught me, more than anybody else ever has, how to become a better writer. To be less sloppy, which I was. I was a pretty good writer in the midst of many scientists, some who really don't like to write much. But I had a lot to learn.

And through it all I felt Dad ever so strongly. The journey felt so much like one Dad and I took together. In fact, when I reached the end, I felt loss and looked forward to continuing to edit and rewrite. And now, I only wish he could read it with me. But I feel thankful to have imagined this opportunity, and to have felt so compelled to focus on these stories as I recognize just how lucky I am to have had the Dad I did.

Sources

Chapter 1: Lover of Rivers
  The Willamette: The story of Oregon's green river. Erin Axelrod, Honor's thesis, Davidson Honor's College, University of Montana

Chapter 2: Snow and Ice
  Journal of Joseph. K. Gill, unpublished, 1884-1931

Chapter 4: Summer
  Pollution in Paradise, Tom McCall, https://oregonencyclopedia.org/articles/pollution_in_paradise_documentary/#.V9acPfBHarU
  Tualatin in the 1960's, Loyce Martinazzi, Tualatin Historical Society

Chapter 6: The Falls
  The White-Headed Eagle, Richard G. Montgomery, 1934, The McMillan Company
  Journal, Chloe Clarke, Willamette University, Hatfield Research Library. Online at: http://libmedia.willamette.edu/cview/archives.html#!doc:page:manuscripts/1645
  Richard G. Montgomery and Frances Anne Interviews, 1974, Oregon Historical Society
  Marion County History Volume XV, Marion County Historical Society, 1998
  Jason Lee: Prophet of the New Oregon, 1985. Academy Books, Portland
  OR
  List of Settlers West of Rockies, 1842, By Elijah White, Indian Agent. From Letters Received by the Office of Indian Affairs, 1842-1880. (Oregon Superintendency)
  http://www.rootsweb.ancestry.com/~orspmhs/18421st.html
  Clackamas County Historic Context Statement, 1990
  http://www.oregon.gov/oprd/HCD/OHC/docs/clackamas_clackamascounty_historicontext_1990.pdf
  History of Oregon Methodism http://archive.org/stream historyoforegonm01yarn historyoforegonm01yarn_djvu.txt
  History of Oregon by Charles Henry Carey https://books.google.com/books?id=nfoXAAAAYAAJ&pg=PA407#v=onepage&q&f=false

Chapter 8: Our Town
City on the Willamette, Percy Maddux, 1952, Binfords & Mort,
Publishers, Portland, OR
Willamette Landings, Howard McKinley Corning, 1947, Oregon
Historical Society

Chapter 10: Boats, Carps and Steamers
Portland's Maritime History, Harrison & Cowan, Arcadia Publishing, 2014
Nuts and Bolts, Journal of Samuel Gill, Hatfield Research Library,
Oregon History Museum
Memories of Steamboat Days, Samuel Gill, Hatfield Research Library,
Oregon History Museum

Chapter 11: Pirates
*Observing Our Peninsula's Past: The Age of Legends through 1931; Volume
One of the Chinook Observer Centennial Project*, Nancy Lloyd, 2003

Chapter 13: Champoeg
Men of Champoeg, Caroline C. Dobbs, 1932, Metropolitan Press
Publishers, Portland OR
The Oregon Memorial of 1838 in the Oregon Historical Quarterly for
March 1933
https://journals.lib.washington.edu/index.php/WHQ/article/
viewFile/8658/7693

Chapter 15: Chemeketa
History of Willamette, Willamette University, http://willamette.edu/
about/history/
Oregon and its Institutions, Reynolds Historical Genealogy Collection
https://archive.org/stream/oregonitsinstitu00hine/
oregonitsinstitu00hine_djvu.txt
How Salem got its Name. Salem Online History
http://www.salemhistory.net/brief_history/salem_name.htm
The Return of Jason Lee, Hatfield Library News, Willamette University,
2015,http://library.willamette.edu/wordpress/archives/author/
mmcrobin/

Chapter 16: Books
Gill's Dictionary of the Chinook Jargon, 15th Edition, 1909, The J.K. Gill
Company, https://archive.org/details/gillsdictionary00goog

Chapter 17: Interrupted
Douglas-fir Tussock Moth in the Blue Mountains, Compiled by David C.
Powell June 2008 https://fs.usda.gov/Internet/FSE_DOCUMENTS/
fsbdev7_015646.pdf
Chloe dusts her Mantel, Frances Gill, 1935, The Press of the Pioneers

Dede Montgomery is a six-generation Oregonian and a certified industrial hygienist working in research at Oregon Health & Science University, where she blogs in *Oregon and the Workplace*. Dede's family ties have instilled in her a deep connection to the land, and curiosity about life in early Oregon and the stories, good and bad, that lay there. In her book, Dede explores the jumbled path of forgiveness, reconciliation, courage and gratitude, through the memories and stories stirred after her father's death. Dede lives with her husband in West Linn, Oregon where she never tires of exploring new places along the banks of the Willamette River. Dede chronicles her life as an Oregonian in her blog, *Musings on Life in Oregon*.

CPSIA information can be obtained
at www.ICGtesting.com
Printed in the USA
FFHW02n1103070918
48244945-52009FF